We Celebrate Confirmation

Rev. William J. Koplik

Joan E. Brady

SILVER BURDETT & GINN
MORRISTOWN, NJ

ACKNOWLEDGMENTS

Scripture selections are from *The New American Bible with Revised New Testament,* © 1986 by the Confraternity of Christian Doctrine, Washington, D.C., and are used with permission. All rights reserved.

Witness of Rev. Viale courtesy *Reflections,* Cathedral Healthcare System, Newark, N.J.

Witness of Joan Callahan excerpted from an article by Mary Ann Weston. Witness of Ethel Williams excerpted from an article by Tricia Gallagher Hempel. Excerpted with permission from *Salt* magazine, published by Claretian Publications: 205 West Monroe St., Chicago, IL 60606.

Excerpts from the English translation of the *Rite of Baptism,* © 1969 International Committee on English in the Liturgy, Inc. (ICEL); *Rite of Confirmation,* © 1975 ICEL; *The Roman Missal,* © 1973 ICEL are used by permission. All rights reserved.

Excerpt from *Sharing the Light of Faith, National Catechetical Directory for Catholics of the United States,* © 1979 by the United States Catholic Conference, Department of Education, Washington, D.C., is used with permission. All rights reserved.

Photo Credits
Photographs by Treehaus Communications, Inc./ Pottebaum except as noted.

8: r. Patterson Graphics, Inc. 12-13: Elizabeth Crews/The Image Works. 14: r. Sara Waskuch. 16: Patterson Graphics, Inc. 17: Patterson Graphics, Inc. 18: t. Tonna Associates for Silver Burdett & Ginn. 18: b. Patterson Graphics, Inc. 20: r. Courtesy of *Catechist.* 24-25: t.r. Sara Waskuch. 25: Sara Waskuch. 31: r. Archdiocese of Newark. 32: Andy Snow. 36-37: Silver Burdett & Ginn. 41: r. Sara Waskuch. 43: l. Andy Snow. 48: l. Daniel De Wilde. 50: t.r. Bob Daemmrich/ The Image Works. 55: r. Sara Waskuch. 62: Bob Morton/St. John Vianney. 63: t.r. Patterson Graphics, Inc.; b.l. Bob Morton/St. John Vianney. 74: t. Mark Antman/The Image Works. 75: t. Martin M. Rotker/TAURUS PHOTOS, INC.; c. Eastcott/ Momatiuk/The Image Works. 78: b.l. Perrin/ Tardy/Gamma Liaison; b.r. Brent Jones. 79: t.r. Michael R. Brown. 82: t.r. Lenore Weber/TAURUS PHOTOS, INC. 83: c.l. CLICK/Chicago. 84: t.r. Julian B. Fasano.

Nihil Obstat:
Kathleen Flanagan, S.C.
Censor Librorum

Imprimatur
✠ Most Reverend Frank J. Rodimer
Bishop of Paterson
January 3, 1989

The **nihil obstat** and **imprimatur** are official declarations that a book or pamphlet is free of doctrinal or moral error. No implication is contained therein that those who granted the **nihil obstat** and **imprimatur** agree with the content, opinions, or statements expressed.

The contents and approach of the *We Celebrate Confirmation* program are in accord with *Basic Teachings for Catholic Religious Education;* the *Rite of Confirmation* and the *Rite of Christian Initiation of Adults,* issued by the National Conference of Catholic Bishops; the *General Catechetical Directory,* issued by the Sacred Congregation for the Clergy; and *Sharing the Light of Faith: National Catechetical Directory for Catholics of the United States,* issued by the United States Catholic Conference.

ABOUT THE AUTHORS

William J. Koplik

William J. Koplik is a priest of the Archdiocese of Newark. He is pastor of Saint Matthew's in Ridgefield, New Jersey. After his ordination in 1962, Father Koplik did graduate studies in religious education at Fordham University. His other published works include three years of Lenten programs based on the liturgical cycles: *Pilgrimage To Promise, Coming To Christ,* and *Forward In Faith.* His articles have appeared in *Ecumenical Essays, Religion Teacher's Journal, Parish Alive, Catechist,* and *Today's Parish.* He is also the coauthor of *Celebrating Forgiveness* and *We Celebrate Baptism.*

Joan E. Brady

Joan E. Brady holds a master's degree in religious education and has done post-graduate work at Fordham University. She is director of religious education in a parish in New Jersey. She is an elected representative to the Executive Board of National Directors and Coordinators of the N.C.E.A. She was president of the Coordinators' Community of the Archdiocese of Newark. Ms. Brady has taught on the junior high school level and has conducted teacher training sessions on sacramental initiation. Her other published works include three books of daily meditations for Advent and Lent: *Light the Darkness; Promise, Patience, and Praise;* and *Journey in Prayer Through Scripture.* Her articles have appeared in *Religion Teacher's Journal, Catechist,* and *Today's Parish.* She is also the coauthor of *Celebrating Forgiveness* and *We Celebrate Baptism.* Ms. Brady lives with her adopted daughter, Rosita.

DEAR CONFIRMATION CANDIDATE,
Welcome! Welcome to a new stage in your journey of faith!

As you prepare to receive the sacrament of Confirmation, take this opportunity to discover more about yourself and learn more about the challenges and joys of being a mature Christian.

At your Baptism, you were first welcomed into the Church. You received the gift of the Holy Spirit to help you grow in Christian faith and love. Your life in Jesus Christ and in the Christian community has been nourished every time you received the Eucharist.

Your Confirmation will further strengthen you to greet the opportunities and conflicts of our world by looking for ways to make it a better place. In Confirmation you will receive in a new way the gift of the Holy Spirit, helping you to be an active, prayerful Christian. The gift of the Spirit helps you to care about and serve others and to give witness to the gospel.

During the rite of Confirmation, you will renew the promises made for you at your Baptism. The gift of the Spirit renews the Church by stirring up the hearts of each individual member. The Spirit comes in a new way to each person to change our lives and the life of the Church.

In this time of preparation you will be making decisions about your commitment as a Christian. You will be involved in an experience of service to others. Your experiences will be very personal as you make decisions that will affect your own life. You will also experience a sense of community with others. Your sense of what it means to be an active member of the Church will develop through your prayer, study, and service. All of this leads to your becoming a fully initiated member of the Body of Christ.

To all of this, welcome!

Father Koplik   Joan E. Brady

 **TABLE OF CONTENTS**

OUR JOURNEY BEGINS

What challenges are you working
to meet in your life?

SHARING JESUS' MISSION

LIFE is full of mysteries, among them, how people grow and change in a world of opportunity, risk, and temptation. Life is full of things to enjoy and think about— favorite music, friends, adventure, ocean tides, dreams. Some things in life help us live together in peace, such as laws. Some things help us appreciate beauty, such as the natural world and works of art.

Life is full of beginnings—puppies and kittens, a baby's first step, a new friend's great smile, the first soccer game, a pair of skates. The mystery of life did not begin with us. What is wonderful is that we are alive now and our lives are full of choices. Life is full of hopes for today and dreams for tomorrow. All beginnings in life are opportunities for us to be more fully alive.

You are at a new point of beginning. You are growing into adulthood. You are beginning to make choices about the kind of person you wish to become.

As you prepare for Confirmation, you can choose for yourself how you want to live as a Christian. You can consider what the sacrament of Confirmation will mean in your life.

Navaho father with baby, St. Michaels Association for Special Education, Window Rock, Arizona

Confirmation

What is **Confirmation*** all about? Confirmation is about you and Jesus. It is about making a difference. Confirmation helps you make the commitment to be a Christian in today's world. Confirmation means making a difference in the lives of others because you care. Confirmation is about the rest of your life. It is knowing that Jesus is with us in his Spirit every step of the way.

Confirmation is about you because what you can do depends on the unique person you are and the talents you possess. Jesus blends all of our gifts together in the Christian community we call the Church. You can help do the work of Jesus!

DISCOVERING QUALITIES

Mark the words that best describe the qualities you admire in others.

_____ practical   _____ strong

_____ creative   _____ easy to talk to

_____ good friend   _____ caring

_____ quick to act   _____ good leader

_____ helping   _____ outgoing

_____ shows courage   _____ good at sports

_____ gentle   _____ aggressive

DESCRIBING YOURSELF

What kind of person are you? What words would your friends use to describe you? How would you describe yourself? You can begin by saying, "I am a person. I belong to a family. In certain ways, I am like other people. In other ways, I am different."

Write several words to describe yourself.

_____

_____

_____

Write a statement that tells how you would like the others in your class to know you.

_____

_____

_____

_____

*Words in bold appear in the glossary pages 96-97.

CHOOSING VALUES

Those things that are important to us we call values. From the following list, choose the values that are most important to you. Rate each value from 1 to 5. Consider the number 1 as being least important and the number 5 as most important. Circle the number you choose for each value.

being loved

1 2 3 4 5

being trusted

1 2 3 4 5

having enough to eat

1 2 3 4 5

being good-looking

1 2 3 4 5

having good friends

1 2 3 4 5

feeling like I belong

1 2 3 4 5

having privacy

1 2 3 4 5

being happy with myself

1 2 3 4 5

playing sports

1 2 3 4 5

having someone to protect me

1 2 3 4 5

having a pet

1 2 3 4 5

having enough money

1 2 3 4 5

doing well in school

1 2 3 4 5

being popular

1 2 3 4 5

A time to be born
and a time to die . . .
A time to weep,
and a time to laugh
Ecclesiastes 3:2-4

WHAT ARE JESUS' VALUES?

In the gospel, we read these words of Jesus: "I came so that they might have life and have it more abundantly" (John 10:10).

What did Jesus mean by the word *life*? Jesus' words and deeds in the gospels can help us understand. Jesus said he came "to bring glad tidings to the poor . . . to proclaim liberty to captives and recovery of sight to the blind, to let the oppressed go free" (Luke 4:18).

Jesus cared for everyone he met. When Jairus begged him to heal his dying daughter, Jesus responded.

> **When he arrived at the house . . . all were weeping and mourning for her, when he said, "Do not weep any longer, for she is not dead, but sleeping." And they ridiculed him, because they knew she was dead. But he took her by the hand and called to her, "Child, arise!" Her breath returned and she immediately arose.**
> *Luke 8:51–55*

UNDERSTANDING JESUS

How do you understand these words of Jesus? Write a statement about Jesus that tells what values you think were important to him.

_____

_____

_____

_____

_____

_____

Jesus shared life with others. In his heart were faith in God as loving creator and love for all people as brothers and sisters. By making life better for others, Jesus showed us how to love. He showed us the way to God's life. When Jesus spoke, he offered hope and encouragement. When he forgave a person, he offered the beginning of a better life. His great command to his followers was to love God and one another.

Left:
Black Heritage Festival
Dayton, Ohio

Above:
Marijane Ryan, founder
of St. Michaels Association for
Special Education, with
Navaho Children

Finding New Life

The apostles were attracted to Jesus by the way he lived. With his death on the cross, they feared that his life and much of their own hopes had ended. They felt emptiness where before they had lived in hope.

Then came the resurrection! God released Jesus from death to glorious new life. Jesus was transformed into the risen Christ—more alive, more present to those he loved than ever before. Life does not end in death! God brings us to new fullness of life. Through faith and love, the apostles could share this life with their risen Lord. Their hearts were joyful. They would tell others the message of Jesus. The good work begun by Jesus would live on through them.

Jesus shares his life with us today so that we may share life with others. Jesus' values are important to us. We do want to forgive those who hurt us. Sometimes it is very difficult to stand up for what we believe in. We might feel shy or frightened. Jesus strengthens us to live in the ways that he showed us.

We experience the richness of life when our faith is strong and our love overflows to touch the lives of others. You might ask yourself whether your list of values reflects faith in Jesus and love for others.

Faithful Love

After Jesus had returned to the Father, his apostles joyfully spread the good news of Jesus. They showed people how to live in faith and love. Many people eagerly accepted the good news and began to live in the new way. Those who believed in the resurrection of Jesus gradually formed communities that today we call the Church.

The early Church proclaimed that Jesus is alive. In Paul's letters to the early Christians, his primary message is the resurrection. To the people of the church he had founded at Corinth, a major Greek city, Paul wrote, "And if Christ has not been raised, then empty is our preaching; empty, too, your faith" (1 Corinthians 15:14).

Today, the faith and teaching of the Church continue to be centered in the resurrection of Jesus. The Church speaks about our life in Christ and celebrates that life through the sacraments.

Sharing New Life with Christ

Your birth was a most important day for many people. You were born or adopted into a family. You are related to people in different ways. You are a son or daughter, a sister or brother, a grandchild, a niece, a nephew, a cousin.

When I was born, I was given the name

_____ .

Your parents chose your name. The day you were baptized was also a most important day. You were called by this name when your parents brought you to the church for **Baptism.** You may choose to be called by this same name by the **bishop** at your Confirmation. In choosing this same name, you affirm your Baptism. To affirm your Baptism is to agree to accept the promises made for you.

You were welcomed into new life in Jesus Christ through your Baptism. You share in life with Jesus and the people in the Church through the sacraments. During the baptismal ceremony, the priest called you by name and said,

> **The Christian community welcomes you with great joy. In its name I claim you for Christ our Savior by the sign of the cross. I now trace the cross on your forehead, and invite your parents (and godparents) to do the same.**

The priest, your parents, and godparents were happy that you were baptized. They represented the Christian community that welcomed you with joy. As you continue your preparation for Confirmation, you may come to be more aware of how people in your parish share Christ's life with you.

If you were baptized as a baby, the decision to share in the life of Christ through Baptism was not yours. It may have been your parents who decided to have you baptized.

They wanted you to grow in the faith that was theirs. During the baptismal ceremony your parents and godparents spoke the promises of Baptism for you.

The priest poured water over your forehead and called you by name as he pronounced the words:

I baptize you in the name of the Father, and of the Son, and of the Holy Spirit.

The priest anointed your head with holy **chrism** (oil) and said,

God the Father of our Lord Jesus Christ has freed you from sin, given you a new birth by water and the Holy Spirit, and welcomed you into his holy people. He now anoints you with the chrism of salvation. As Christ was anointed Priest, Prophet, and King, so may you live always as a member of his body, sharing everlasting life.

BAPTISM RECORD

I was baptized on

_____ , 19____.

I was baptized at

_____

Church.

The name I received at Baptism was

_____ .

My sponsors at Baptism were

_____

and _____ .

At Baptism

_____

spoke in my name.

At Confirmation

_____

will speak for _____ .

CHOOSING TO BE CONFIRMED

If you decide to publicly affirm your Christian faith in the sacrament of Confirmation, you will be enrolled as a candidate. The Enrollment Promise certificate states what is expected of you. When you have read this, you can decide whether you want to commit yourself in Confirmation to the promises made in your name at Baptism.

If you choose to become a candidate for the sacrament of Confirmation, you will be asked to attend several learning sessions. There you will be helped to understand what Confirmation is. You will have a chance to talk about what the sacrament means to you. You will take part in special celebrations that will help you better appreciate what belonging to the Church means.

CANDIDATE FOR CONFIRMATION

Write a statement telling why you want to be a candidate for the sacrament of Confirmation.

_____

_____

_____

_____

_____

_____

_____

_____

_____

_____

_____

_____

Welcoming Babies

The sun streaming in through the bedroom window shone brightly on the infant in the crib. The baby began to stir and murmur. Eighteen-year-old Liz, who was home from college, tiptoed into the baby's room. She looked at little Christopher. He looked up at Liz and began to cry. Liz gently picked him up.

Christopher is one of the many infants who have come to stay with the Herr family during the past nine years. These have all been babies who needed what the agencies call a "temporary care family" while they were waiting for other families to adopt them. Now three weeks old, Christopher came to the Herr family right from the hospital, as did most of the other babies. The family members love him as if he will be with them forever. However, even as they cuddle him and play with him, they know at any time his permanent home may be ready.

Some of the infants have stayed for just a few weeks. Others have stayed for several months. Each baby needed a loving temporary home, during which time they awaited adoption into a permanent home. This is the gift the Herrs as a family have chosen to provide.

About ten years ago, Mary and Tom, along with their four daughters, answered a plea made by Catholic Charities in Chicago for temporary care families. Their youngest daughter was two at the time. The Herrs discussed becoming a temporary care family. They decided that this was a gift they could all give. They were one of only two families that responded to this need. This was a way that they as a family could respond to the gospel message, "When I was homeless you opened your door." Since the Herr family responded to this call, their home has regularly had an infant boy or girl.

This is a family project, so they all help to care for the babies. Tom and the girls take turns with baby care at night so that Mary can rest. Most of the time Mary handles the daytime care of each new member of the family.

Saying good-bye to a baby is always difficult. Each new baby means a new beginning — for both the family and the baby. Mary keeps a diary for each baby. She then hands this diary on to the adoptive parents. The new parents can enjoy reading the story of the first weeks of their baby's life.

The Herrs have chosen to give the most vulnerable in our society a loving home when they need it. As these children begin their life on earth, they receive the loving care they need.

Leader: Most of us were baptized when we were too young to affirm our faith in Christ for ourselves. Now as we prepare for the sacrament of Confirmation, we are asked to speak for ourselves, to declare our faith in Jesus and his Church.

Let us pray for guidance as we think about our lives and our readiness to assume the responsibilities of full members of the Church.

Student 1: Lord, you know everything about us—not only what we do and say, but the secrets that we cherish in our hearts and the feelings that we sometimes hide.

All: Lord Jesus, help us prepare to share more fully in your life.

Student 2: Lord, you are always there to understand our doubts and fears, our anger and frustration.

All: Lord Jesus, help us prepare to share more fully in your life.

Student 3: Lord, our lives are not easy. Sometimes it seems as if we cannot do anything right, but you always have confidence in us.

All: Lord Jesus, help us prepare to share more fully in your life.

Leader: Lord, these words and symbols of our lives represent us. Guide us as we begin to prepare for Confirmation.

All: Lord Jesus, help us prepare to share more fully in your life.

Leader: Creator,
send us your Holy Spirit
to help us walk in faith
and grow to become more
like your Son, Jesus Christ,
who lives and reigns with you
and the Holy Spirit,
one God, for ever and ever.

All: Amen.

REVIEWING: OUR JOURNEY BEGINS

Crossword Puzzle Remembering what you learned, work the puzzle.

Across

1. Sacrament that affirms your Christian faith
5. Baptism and Confirmation are two of the seven _____
6. Clergyman who often confers the sacrament of Baptism
8. The great commandment of Jesus is to _____
10. The friends of Jesus who first experienced his new life
12. Someone preparing for Confirmation is called a _____

Down

1. Used for anointing in Baptism and Confirmation
2. In Confirmation, you publicly affirm your Christian _____
3. The new life of Jesus
4. Clergyman who usually confers Confirmation
7. Who shows us the way to God's life
9. Persons who chose to have you baptized
11. Jesus said he came to bring us new _____

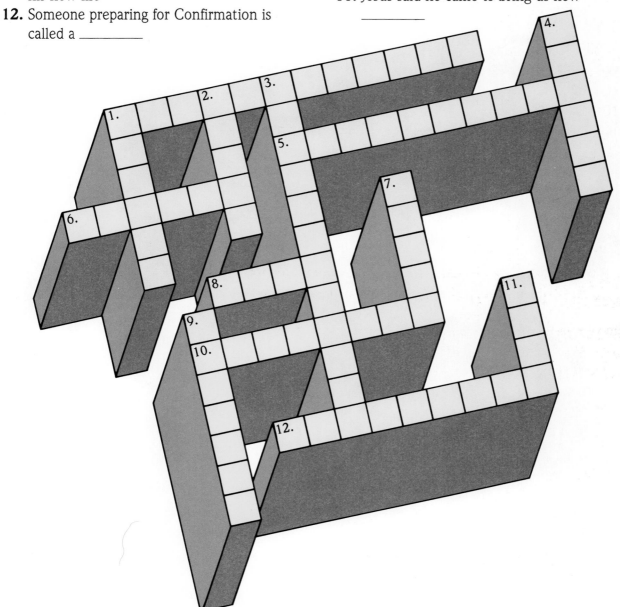

GROWING AS CHRISTIANS

What do you enjoy doing
with a group of friends?

BELONGING

A SENSE of belonging is important. Everyone needs to belong. Have you wanted to join a team, club, or organization in your town? Why did you want to be a member? How did you first learn about the group? How did you come to join it?

Have you moved into a new neighborhood, a new school, or a new parish? Who was the first person you met? When did you begin to feel that you belonged?

There are steps to joining a group. First you learn about the group. You learn what its goals are. Even groups of friends have goals. Some groups of friends like to play sports. Other groups go to the movies. Some groups just "hang out." You may find that it is identified by a special greeting, a motto, or a combination of colors. Some of your friends may already be members. You ask to join.

BELONGING TO A GROUP

What is one group you belong to?

_____ .

Tell how you became a member.

_____ .

_____ .

Its purpose is _____ .

_____ .

People can identify its members by

_____ .

I like belonging to this group because

_____ .

MEMBERSHIP IN THE CHURCH

During the early years of the Church, people became members in stages. First they asked to belong to the Church. They were called **catechumens**. They studied to prepare themselves to be good members.

When the catechumens completed their preparation and were ready to become full members, they participated in a rite of initiation in which they were welcomed into the community in three sacred actions. During the ritual, the catechumens were first baptized by water and the Spirit. Next, they were anointed with chrism. Finally, the catechumens were welcomed to the eucharistic table, where they received the body and blood of Jesus for the first time.

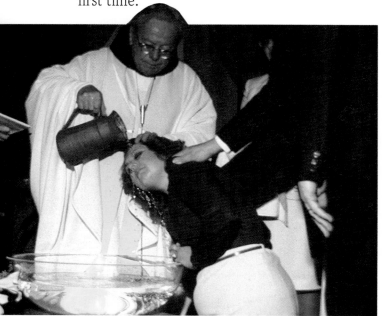

Today, these stages make up the three separate sacraments of Baptism, Confirmation, and **Eucharist.** Today people may also be initiated in the manner of the early Christians. In many parishes people are welcomed in stages. The final stage can include the sacraments of Baptism, Confirmation, and Eucharist, and often occurs during the Easter Vigil on the night before Easter. This process is called the **Rite of Christian Initiation.**

You are preparing to take on a new role in the Christian community.
Like the **catechumens**, you will be asked
- to learn about your faith
- to practice your faith through service
- to worship with the community

The **sacraments of initiation**—Baptism, Confirmation, and the Eucharist—help us experience a closer relationship with Jesus and with other people. The water and the words of Baptism mark the beginning of life as a Christian. In the anointing of Confirmation, the Holy Spirit strengthens us. We receive power to show by our way of life that we are followers of Jesus. Receiving the Eucharist brings us into close fellowship with Jesus and with others who accept him as Lord. Through these sacraments we become more fully part of the **Body of Christ**.

Auxiliary Bishop Peter A. Rosazza of Hartford, Conn.

Strengthening Your Membership

Preparing for Confirmation will help you better understand the Church and live as a member. The sacrament of Confirmation will help you to love and serve others. The bishop or his representative will confirm you because the bishop is the leader of the **diocese.** He speaks for the larger Church community to which you are called to belong.

Ideally the sacrament of Confirmation is celebrated within the Eucharist. When we receive the bread of life, we share with others all that we believe about Jesus. We are strengthened to bring Jesus to all we meet.

At the celebration of the Eucharist, the rite of Confirmation follows the reading of the gospel.

Rite of Confirmation

The rite of Confirmation begins as the candidates are presented to the bishop. This introduction is made by your pastor or by one of the other priests of your parish. Or your catechist might introduce you. You may be called by name, or you may be called as a member of the group.

When you stand before the bishop, you will publicly show that you believe in Jesus and want to follow him. This will be a significant time for you. You will be doing something you choose to do after thinking and praying about being confirmed.

Homily

The bishop will welcome the candidates and their families. He will congratulate them, as well as the teachers, the priests of the parish, and all who helped the candidates. Confirmation is a time for rejoicing. It brings together the people of the parish in the celebration of one faith.

The bishop will give a brief **homily,** or instruction. It may be based on the readings of the Confirmation Mass. The coming of the Holy Spirit to the apostles at **Pentecost** is often part of the bishop's homily. The apostles received the gift of the Holy Spirit at Pentecost. The bishop

may describe how eagerly and joyfully they responded to the presence of the Spirit in their lives, and he might explain why Pentecost is remembered at Confirmation.

THE FIRST PENTECOST

Read the story of Pentecost in the Acts of the Apostles 2:1–41. Answer the questions.

What did the apostles experience on that first Pentecost?

_____

_____

How did the apostles respond to that experience?

_____

_____

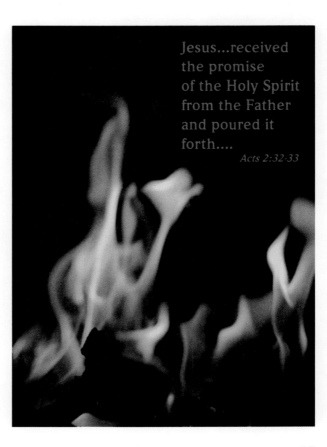

Jesus...received the promise of the Holy Spirit from the Father and poured it forth....

Acts 2:32-33

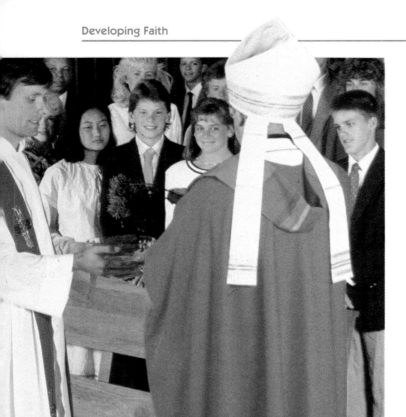

Renewal of Baptismal Promises

At Baptism your parents and sponsors spoke in your name. They made promises and expressed their faith. They asked that you share in the faith that they professed. In Confirmation you will affirm your Baptism. The bishop will ask you to respond for yourself. He will ask you to renew the promises that were made for you at Baptism and to profess your faith. He will ask you to respond to the following questions with, "I do."

RENEWAL OF BAPTISMAL PROMISES

Write in your responses to these questions.

Do you reject Satan and all his works

and all his empty promises?_____

Do you believe in God the Father almighty,

creator of heaven and earth? _____

**Do you believe in Jesus Christ, his only Son,
  our Lord,**
who was born of the Virgin Mary,
was crucified, died, and was buried,
rose from the dead,
and is now seated at the right hand of the

Father? _____

Do you believe in the Holy Spirit,
the Lord, the giver of life,
who came upon the apostles at Pentecost
and today is given to you sacramentally in

confirmation? _____

**Do you believe in the holy catholic Church,
The communion of saints, the forgiveness
of sins, the resurrection of the body, and life**

everlasting? _____

Then the bishop will say, **This is our faith.
This is the faith of the Church. We are proud
to profess it in Christ Jesus our Lord.**

You will answer, "Amen" with all present at the ceremony. *Amen* means "so it is," "surely," or "I agree with that." You will be saying yes to the bishop's words about our faith.

The bishop will extend his hands over all those to be confirmed. This gesture is called the laying on of hands. It is a very old practice. Both the Hebrew Scriptures and the Christian Scriptures record that the laying on of hands was used when a person was dedicated to God for a certain task. At Confirmation, the laying on of hands signifies that the power of the Holy Spirit is given to each candidate.

At the laying on of hands, the bishop will pray that you will receive the gift of the Spirit in a special way. He will pray the following prayer.

The Laying on of Hands

After all the people present renew the promises made at Baptism, the bishop will pray the following prayer.

> My dear friends:
> in baptism God our Father gave the new
>   birth of eternal life
> to his chosen sons and daughters.
> Let us pray to our Father
> that he will pour out the Holy Spirit
> to strengthen his sons and daughters with
>   his gifts
> and anoint them to be more like Christ
>   the Son of God.

During the brief silence that will follow that prayer, you might reflect on your baptismal promises and the Holy Spirit being present in your life. You might think of ways in which you could be more like Christ.

> All-powerful God, Father of our Lord
>   Jesus Christ,
> by water and the Holy Spirit
> you freed your sons and daughters from
> sin and gave them new life.
> Send your Holy Spirit upon them
> to be their Helper and Guide.
> Give them the spirit of wisdom
>   and understanding,
> the spirit of right judgment and courage,
> the spirit of knowledge and reverence.
> Fill them with the spirit of wonder and
>   awe in your presence.
> We ask this through Christ our Lord.

The Anointing with Chrism

After the laying on of hands, each person to be confirmed will be presented, in turn, to the bishop. The presentation is made by a **sponsor** or sponsors.

Sponsors represent all the people of the Church. By being present they are saying to those who are about to be confirmed, "The members of the Church want you to know that we support you. We want to share our Christian faith with you. We will be happy to guide you as you try daily to live the words of Jesus."

You will step forward with your sponsor or sponsors to receive a special sacramental sign and to hear the words of the sacrament of Confirmation. This sacramental sign is an anointing with oil, or chrism. Chrism is a mixture of oil and balsam. This tradition, like the laying on of hands, is also very old. In ancient Israel the practice had many significant meanings. Its religious meaning was to signify that a person was being set apart from others and given a special mission. The Bible tells us that Solomon was anointed when he became king.

The oil is absorbed into the anointed person and becomes a part of that person. The Hebrew word *Messiah* means "anointed one." The Greek word *Christos,* or *Christ,* also means "anointed one." Anointing is a sign that tells me I am to become Christ for others.

When you step forward and stand before the bishop to be confirmed, he will moisten his right thumb with chrism. He will then place his hand on your head and make the sign of the cross with his thumb on your forehead. At this time, he will address you by name and say the words of Confirmation: **Be sealed with the Gift of the Holy Spirit.**

After your response, "Amen," the bishop will then say to you, "Peace be with you." As a newly confirmed member of the Church, your response is, "And also with you."

General Intercessions

You may then take your place in the congregation as a newly-confirmed member of the Church. With all the people who are present, you will pray for the needs of the Church. Those prayers are called the General Intercessions. After the intercessions, the **liturgy** will continue.

Look at the prayer on page 17 that the bishop prays as he extends his hands. Write the gifts of the Spirit named in that prayer.

1. _____   2. _____

3. _____   4. _____

5. _____   6. _____

7. _____

The gifts of the Holy Spirit are not magic powers that will change you on the day of your Confirmation. The gifts of the Holy Spirit are life-giving qualities that help you become the person God calls you to be. Your birth in the Holy Spirit through Baptism is strengthened in you through Confirmation. By receiving the Holy Spirit anew in Confirmation, you are helped to become a more loving person, a kinder person, a more understanding person.

DECISIONS TO BE MADE

You know about the ceremony in which a person is confirmed. You have some decisions to make that you should now begin to think about. There is, of course, the all-important decision to want to affirm your faith as a Christian. There is a decision to be made about your name. Another decision concerns your sponsor or sponsors. Still another decision concerns your part in the Confirmation ceremony.

When the bishop confirms you, he will call you by name. Your name identifies you. It is a part of who you are.

The Church suggests that we use our baptismal names at Confirmation to show that Baptism and Confirmation are closely related. But if for some reason a candidate wishes to choose a new name at Confirmation, he or she

is free to do so. You should begin to think about the name you wish to use.

As I receive Confirmation, I wish to be called

_____ .

During the Confirmation ceremony, the people who accept you as a newly confirmed member of the Church are represented by a sponsor or sponsors. A sponsor is a person who presents you to the bishop to be anointed with chrism. You may choose one person to be your sponsor, or you may choose two people to stand with you before the bishop.

Whom will you choose? You may want to consider people who are special to you because they help you grow in your faith. You may consider your godparents, for they will surely give **witness** to the connection between your Baptism and your Confirmation.

You should think of people you admire for the way they live as mature Catholics, who are active members of the Church. Sponsors should be people who are proud to present you for Confirmation because of your willingness to live the Christian life. You should choose as a sponsor a person who will take an active part in helping you grow in your Christian faith.

Your sponsor should be someone who has already been confirmed in the Catholic faith. You may indicate your choices below.

I wish to have

_____

_____

be my sponsor(s) for Confirmation because

_____

_____ .

Taking Part in the Confirmation

There are many ways in which you can take part in your Confirmation ceremony. You may be asked to help prepare the liturgy. You may want to make a banner to place in the church, or you may help choose the music for the ceremony. You may write a prayer of petition for the Prayer of the Faithful. Perhaps you may read a passage from Scripture during the ceremony, or you may join other newly confirmed persons in taking the gifts to the altar.

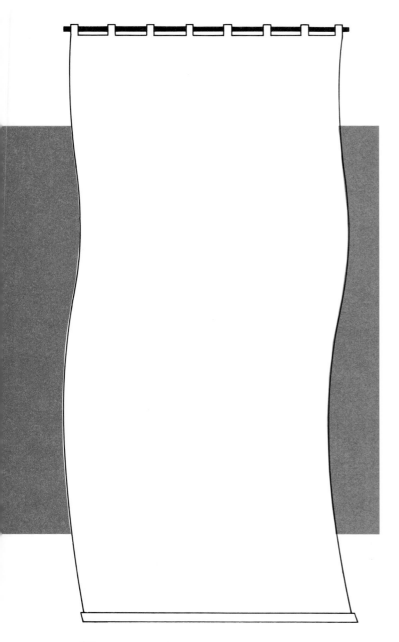

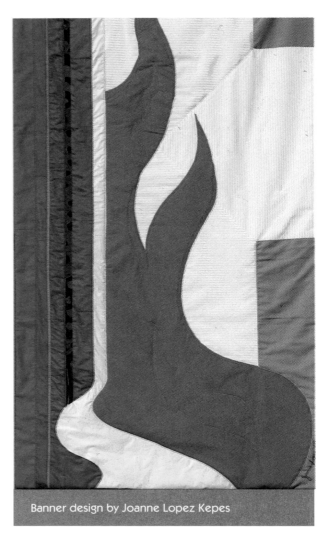

Banner design by Joanne Lopez Kepes

CONFIRMATION SYMBOL

Think of a design or symbol that would represent Confirmation for you. Draw it in the space. You may want to make this into a banner for Confirmation.

YOUR CONTRIBUTION

What would you like to do to help give special meaning to the ceremony in which you will be confirmed?

_____

_____

Healing the Spirit as Well as the Body

Usually, Father Paul Viale begins his working day by praying with the three other chaplains who make up the pastoral care team at Saint Michael's Medical Center in Newark, New Jersey. But this morning Father Paul's day began more abruptly, with a message over his beeper alerting him to a pediatric "Code 8" in the emergency room, a child in cardiac arrest.

"When I got to the ER," Father Paul said, "I found out that a mother had just rushed in her four-month-old baby because he wasn't breathing. There was a whole crowd working on the baby, trying to resuscitate him, so I went to the waiting area to be with the mother. I put my hand on her and just stayed with her. In a situation like that you don't really do or say anything. You're just there."

Close to an hour passed before a doctor and a nurse came out of the room. The news was not good. Although they had tried to resuscitate the infant, they were unsuccessful. The death was the result of a known heart defect the baby had been born with.

"I just held her in my arms and let her cry," Father Paul said. "She was very upset, and she insisted on going into the treatment room to see her baby. But once inside, she wouldn't look. Then Vivian Leahy, an assistant director of nursing, said to her, 'Look at your baby's face. Do you see any pain or suffering there?' The mother looked at her baby and calmed down." Father Paul stayed with the mother until family members came to take her home.

Father Paul's role in that sad event illustrates how the work of pastoral care in a Catholic hospital has changed greatly over the years. "Traditionally," he said, "the approach was very sacramental — giving communion and anointing the sick. Today we do much more counseling. We have to know how to listen; we have to understand the grief process, how to be with families and patients at times of crisis."

At Saint Michael's Father Paul promotes an atmosphere of holistic healing. "That means viewing the spiritual, emotional, and physical aspects of a person as one, and understanding how each of those parts affects the other."

Every day at noon Father Paul celebrates Mass in Saint Michael's chapel. "Patients come in their wheelchairs," he said. "Visitors and staff come. I love being with the patients. As difficult as that sometimes is, that's what Catholic health care ministry is all about."

CELEBRATING: GROWING AS CHRISTIANS

Leader: Lord, we have come to the end of this learning session. It has been filled with a great deal of information. Now we take time out to look to you. We see that becoming a Christian involves much more than information. We need to be formed into a new people, to choose to discover your influence and action in our lives.

Student: (Reads from Jeremiah 18:1–6)

Leader: Lord, we know that just as clay is formed by hand, so too are we formed as your followers. In Confirmation, we will celebrate our desire to continue this formation. Help us to prepare well to receive this sacrament.

All: Just as clay is formed by hand, so too do you act upon us, Lord.

Leader: **God of power and mercy,
send your Holy Spirit to live in our hearts
and make us temples of his glory.
We ask this through our Lord Jesus Christ, your Son,
who lives and reigns with you and the Holy Spirit,
one God, for ever and ever.**

All: **Amen.**

REVIEWING: GROWING AS CHRISTIANS

Fill In the Blanks

Use the clues below to complete the puzzle. The circled letters form a word used in this chapter.

1. During the Confirmation ceremony, the sponsors _____ the candidates to the bishop.
2. A sacrament of initiation that frequently renews our fellowship with Jesus Christ and those who follow him.
3. The _____ on of hands is a gesture the bishop makes as a sign that the power of the Holy Spirit is being given.
4. To tell or show what you have seen or heard
5. Set of symbolic actions
6. A sacrament of initiation in which we are anointed with oil and receive strength from the Holy Spirit
7. A Catholic community made up of many parishes
8. A special sign of Christ's grace and our faith
9. Followers of Jesus who were among the first to receive the gift of the Holy Spirit

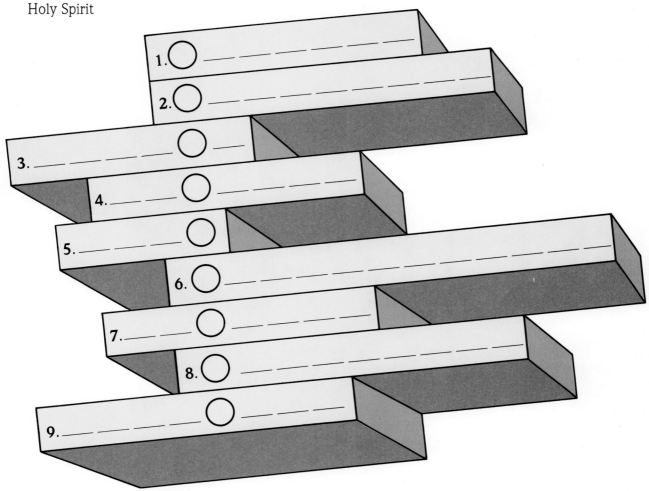

WITNESSING TO JESUS

How do you communicate
something important?

THE POWER OF WORDS

THE words you use are one way of communicating your thoughts, ideas, and feelings to others. Your gestures, the way you move, the look on your face, all help to give your words more meaning. Through words, you express opinions, describe plans, tell others what you know. Your words and expressions show that you are happy or sad, excited or calm, thoughtful or having fun. With words, you can make others laugh, offer comfort, and build friendship.

Sometimes words are used to hurt others. Words can bring disappointment or cause an unfriendly feeling. Words can mislead when they allow others to think something that is not really true.

Sometimes you might want to express what you really think or feel, but in certain situations it may be hard to find just the right words. You might wish another could understand your heart or mind without words.

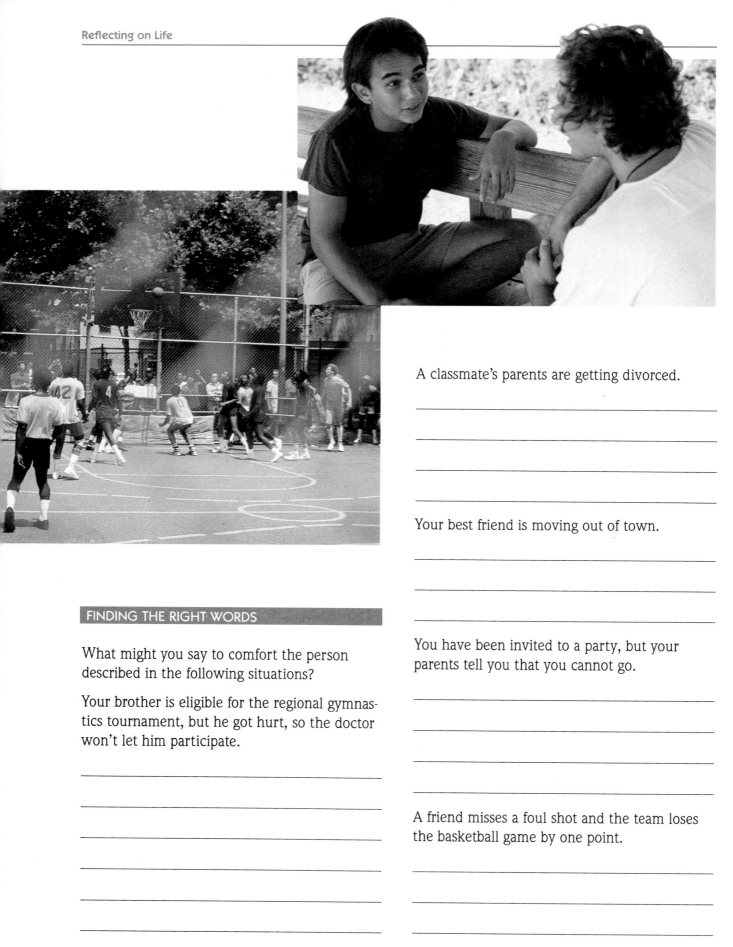

A classmate's parents are getting divorced.

_____

_____

_____

Your best friend is moving out of town.

_____

_____

_____

FINDING THE RIGHT WORDS

What might you say to comfort the person described in the following situations?

Your brother is eligible for the regional gymnastics tournament, but he got hurt, so the doctor won't let him participate.

_____

_____

_____

_____

You have been invited to a party, but your parents tell you that you cannot go.

_____

_____

_____

A friend misses a foul shot and the team loses the basketball game by one point.

_____

_____

SEARCHING FOR MEANING

Perhaps you have had the sad experience of a favorite classmate moving away. Or perhaps you have suffered the loss of someone in your family through death or divorce. When a family or group of friends loses someone to death whom they care about, they often get together to support one another. They share memories of the person who died. In that way, they keep alive the memory of that person.

Though the apostles shared their grief after Jesus died, they did feel troubled. Scripture tells us that the apostles could not always find words to express what Jesus had meant to them. At times, they were not able to show that they believed in Jesus and everything he had taught them.

The way the apostles acted after the death of Jesus makes that clear. Jesus had given them strength and courage by everything he said and did, and when he was no longer with them, they felt sad and confused. However, they remained together in a community.

They remembered what Jesus had taught and tried to live it. They said nothing about Jesus to outsiders because they were fearful that they, too, would die as Jesus had.

The promise Jesus made to the apostles at the Last Supper had not yet come to pass. That promise is found in the gospel of John 14:16–17.

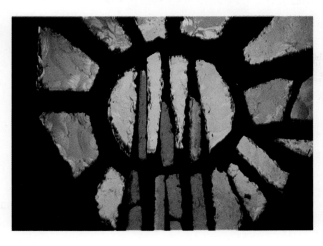

The Promise Is Fulfilled

The promise Jesus made to the apostles to send the Holy Spirit became real to them at a feast we call Pentecost. In Chapter 2 of the Acts of the Apostles, we read that the apostles were together in an upper room of a house one day. They were praying and discussing what had happened in the last days of Jesus' life.

The author Luke describes what happened in the upper room in this way:

> And suddenly there came from the sky a noise like a strong driving wind, and it filled the entire house in which they were. Then there appeared to them tongues as of fire, which parted and came to rest on each one of them. And they were all filled with the holy Spirit and began to speak in different tongues, as the Spirit enabled them to proclaim.
>
> *(Acts 2:3–4)*

Special Olympics, Dayton, Ohio

PRESENCE OF THE SPIRIT

Luke tried to show what the presence of the Holy Spirit was like by referring to wind and fire. Wind is often described in the following ways.

- Wind blows where it will.
- We cannot see the wind, but we can feel its effects.
- Wind brings a change—the gentle breeze of spring or the gusty gale of winter.
- Wind is the breath of life.

Choose two of these examples and write why they describe the Holy Spirit for you.

1. _____

_____

_____

_____

2. _____

_____

_____

_____

Fire is often described by what it does.

- Fire can warm us on a cold night.
- Fire can cook food.
- Fire is attractive and people sometimes gather around it.
- Fire provides a light or a beacon to those who are seeking the way.

Choose two of these examples and write why fire reminds you of the Holy Spirit.

1. _____

_____

_____

2. _____

_____

_____

Can you think of other ways to describe the presence of the Holy Spirit? Why? Write about it.

_____

_____

_____

_____

_____

Transformed by the Promise

At Pentecost the apostles experienced the presence of the Holy Spirit. They were no longer afraid. They could truly say, "We believe in Jesus." They understood Jesus' message in a deeper way; it had come alive for them.

Together they could look back on the words and actions of Jesus that had once confused them. They came to realize more and more what Jesus' life was about. The power of the Holy Spirit opened their minds and hearts in faith.

Now the apostles wanted everyone to know Jesus as they did. Now they were able to put their belief into words. They wanted also to put their words into action. At Pentecost, Peter addressed a large group of people who had gathered outside the house after hearing the loud noise made by the coming of the Spirit.

Peter told them how God had raised Jesus who had been crucified. He spoke to them of Jesus and his message. He proclaimed Jesus as Lord and Messiah. He told them that Jesus is the one who forgives, who helps us overcome difficulties, who fills us with joy, whose loving presence with us even death cannot destroy.

Peter told the people that Jesus' promise to send the Spirit was made for them also. A new and wonderful future awaited all who would receive the Spirit. The people were filled with hope. Peter invited all present to accept the good news of Jesus, to turn from wrongdoing, be baptized, and to receive the **gift of the Spirit**. The gift of the Spirit would help them live in witness to their faith. Read the promise in Acts of the Apostles 2:38.

Repent and be baptized, every one of you, in the name of Jesus Christ for the forgiveness of your sins; and you will receive the gift of the holy Spirit.

Acts 2:38

29

Making Pentecost Present

The Holy Spirit is a mystery: we cannot completely understand who the Spirit is. But there are ways we can help ourselves to think about the Holy Spirit. In the gospels we read that the Holy Spirit is the spirit of God. Can you think of anyone in your life whose spirit stays with you and helps you?

As you go through a difficult medical or dental procedure, perhaps the spirit of a good friend who has suffered in an accident has helped you to cope with your own discomfort. The spirit of your parent might be with you as you face a tough decision at school or at a party. The spirit of a grandparent who has died remains with your family during holiday celebrations. The spirit of a friend who has moved away lives in your heart and can help you with day to day situations.

What is the spirit of Jesus? It is a spirit of great kindness, a spirit of courage in the face of hardships, a spirit of energy in dealing with injustice.

The Spirit will come to you in a new way in the sacrament of Confirmation. This coming of the Holy Spirit may be less dramatic than it was at the first Pentecost. However, it will be just as real and just as important in your life. The Holy Spirit will strengthen you to witness to Christ, in the way you choose to live.

In the Confirmation ceremony, the bishop will pray that everyone present may share in the hope of Pentecost. He says,

**God our Father,
you sent your Holy Spirit upon the apostles,
and through them and their successors you give the Spirit to your people.
May his work begun at Pentecost continue to grow in the hearts of all who believe.
We ask this through Christ our Lord.**

In order to be a witness to the Christian message, you must first understand the message. We read it in the Christian Scriptures. It would be best to have your own copy of the Christian Scriptures so that you can read them and come to understand how a confirmed Christian is expected to live.

Outdoor Mass celebrating 400th anniversary of the Franciscans, Dayton, Ohio

Teens help out in a soup kitchen

WHAT IS EXPECTED OF A CHRISTIAN

In Matthew's gospel we read what Jesus expects of each person who wants to follow him and enter the kingdom of eternal life. Read Matthew 25:31–46. Describe those actions on which Jesus tells us we will be judged.

1. _____

2. _____

3. _____

4. _____

5. _____

6. _____

The following examples show people performing various acts of service. From the list above, write the number of the action described by Jesus that corresponds to each act of service.

A group of high school students helps collect children's clothing to distribute to needy

families at Thanksgiving. _____

A religious sister spends time each week at a women's prison teaching job skills that the

women can use in the future. _____

Two eighth graders spend their free time after lunch preparing bags of food for those who come

to a neighborhood soup kitchen. _____

A woman who has recovered from cancer visits

with cancer patients in a local hospital. _____

A family cares for newborn babies who will be adopted until a permanent home is ready for

them. _____

A high school senior teaches first grade in the

parish religious education program. _____

CHOOSING A WAY TO WITNESS

As you prepare for Confirmation, your parish church might ask that you serve others through a witness experience. Thus, you can show that you believe in Jesus and his message. In this way, the kingdom that Jesus spoke of can become more real to those who receive your care.

Look at your own life. There are probably several ways in which you already live out the gospel message of Jesus. Perhaps you help care for a younger child, or help with dinner, or keep your room neat without being reminded.

Your preparation for Confirmation includes learning about your faith, celebrating your faith, and witnessing to your faith in your daily life. You may choose a specific way to witness to your faith. You might consider the following suggestions in planning your witness experience.

- Help with a special program, such as vacation church school, a Saturday program at the local library, or an after-school park program.

- Mow the lawn or shovel the snow without pay for a senior citizen, a friend's mother, or someone else in need in your neighborhood.

- Volunteer to help with a Special Olympics program in your area.

- Learn of opportunities to help in local homes for the elderly or the disabled.

- Contact your local library to learn if you can help there after school.

- Find out where a soup kitchen or food pantry is located in your area. Explore how you can help.

- Offer your assistance to a local senior citizens group. They might appreciate having a group of young people serve refreshments or help in other ways.

- If your parish celebrates the sacrament of the Anointing of the Sick at a special service, find out if you can help with people in wheelchairs, bring flowers or refreshments, or assist in some other way.

Look around you. The needs that can arise in your area are many. Explore options; then choose a way in which you would like to witness to your understanding of the gospel. As you decide, you might ask yourself some questions.

Do you want to tackle your witness experience by yourself? Do you prefer to work with a group of friends? How much time can you give in service? Can you work on it a few days a week or only on Saturdays? Ask the help of your parents and your teacher as you make these decisions.

Plan your witness experience well so that you can do it well. Remember, if you choose to help someone, plan to persevere in your efforts so that the person's needs can truly be met.

Confirmation strengthens you in your ability to serve others. After Confirmation your service can continue. In looking for ways to help others, you will be saying, "Yes, the gospel message means something to me. Pentecost means something to me. I, too, want to witness to Jesus and to help improve my corner of the world."

Visiting the Homebound

Joan Callahan agreed to take an old lady shopping and ended up adopting a grandmother.

In the winter of 1979, Chicago was immobilized by several feet of snow. Joan set up a neighborhood emergency exchange where residents could help each other. She got a call from Adeline, single and nearly 90, who had lived alone for 43 years despite arthritis and hearing problems.

Joan took Adeline shopping, and "from there our relationship developed," she said. Adeline was full of stories, and Joan enjoyed listening.

"Adeline became like my grandmother, someone I could take care of and feel connected with," Joan said. "I needed that."

When Joan and her husband adopted a baby girl, she kidded Adeline about her adopted grandmother having an adopted granddaughter. "It was nice to share Maureen with Adeline and watch Adeline's joy. She hadn't held a baby in twenty years," Joan said.

Joan Callahan was a social worker in St. Clement's, a Chicago parish. As she worked with the home visitors, Joan saw people's spiritual gifts used where they were most needed.

The home visitors encourage the older people to reminisce about their lives. The elderly need to have a sense of what they have accomplished. Volunteers came away with a new appreciation for the strength, faith, and intelligence of those they visit.

"You don't get to be 85 or 90 without really good skills and strengths," said Joan.

Adeline lived to be 96. In the spring of 1988, Joan and her husband adopted a baby boy, Patrick. Joan wishes that Adeline were still alive so that she could see Patrick.

Today, Joan is involved in a variety of ministries. She directs the hospital eucharistic ministry program of St. Clement's. She provides education and counseling for the parents of boys and girls who are temporarily residing at Mercy Boys and Girls Home because of family crises.

Joan provides counseling for a group of parents of handicapped children at the University of Illinois Hospital. The parents meet to share emotional support and to discuss the stresses and problems they experience in caring for their children.

Joan is on the board of directors and volunteers with the AIDS Pastoral Care Network in Chicago. Volunteers provide spiritual support to people affected by AIDS.

"Retired" now from full-time employment because she is home caring for Maureen and Patrick, Joan finds that her social-work skills are still needed.

CELEBRATING: WITNESSING TO JESUS

Student 1: Lord Jesus, you made a promise to send the Holy Spirit to be our helper and guide. That promise was fulfilled for the apostles at Pentecost. At our Confirmation, the promise of Pentecost will be made real for us. Pentecost will become present for us. We pray that with your help we will be able to make Pentecost present in our own lives.

Student 2: (Reads from 1 Corinthians 12:4–11)

Leader: Together, we can make the mission of Jesus real in the world today. We can be a light to others. We can live together as brothers and sisters who are able to call God "Father."

All: Our Father, who art in heaven,
  hallowed be thy name;
Thy kingdom come, thy will be done
  on earth as it is in heaven.
Give us this day our daily bread;
and forgive us our trespasses
  as we forgive those
  who trespass against us;
and lead us not into temptation,
  but deliver us from evil.

Leader: **Lord,
fulfill your promise:
Send your Holy Spirit to make us
witnesses before the world
to the Good News proclaimed by
Jesus Christ, our Lord,
who lives and reigns with you and
the Holy Spirit,
one God, for ever and ever.**

All: **Amen.**

REVIEWING: **WITNESSING TO JESUS**

Fill In the Blanks

Look at the answers below and choose the correct one for each statement. Write the answer on the line following the statement.

something earned	Christian Scriptures	gift	Hebrew Scriptures
Passover	Paul	Pentecost	Peter
wind and fire	presence of our parents	sand and rocks	presence of the Spirit
service	suggestion	vacation	promise

1. At Pentecost this apostle told a large group of people about Jesus.

____

2. The presence of the Holy Spirit is sometimes described in these ways.

____

3. The apostles were gathered for this Jewish feast when the Holy Spirit came upon them.

____

4. The Holy Spirit comes to those who have faith in Jesus to help us live as Christians. This coming of the Holy Spirit is

______________________________.

5. The section of the Bible that tells about the life of Jesus and his apostles.

____

6. When Jesus said he would send his Spirit to his apostles, he was making a ______________________________.

7. As Christians, we are asked to help others. This is called

______________________________.

8. As Christians, we can trust that we will always have with us the

______________________________.

RESPONDING IN FAITH

What would you like people
to remember about you?

KEEPING YOUR STORY ALIVE

FOR everyone, life holds many memories. Some memories are happy, others might be sad. What happened to you in the past helps to make you the kind of person you are today.

You have celebrated many events in your life. Some you can clearly recall. Of other events, you have vague memories. Yet you might know something about such events from other people's recollections. Perhaps someone has described how you acted on your first birthday, or how you learned to walk or talk.

Some of your family members recall certain events in your life because they were present. Each person recalls events a little bit differently. Is there a humorous event in your past that your family or friends keep alive by retelling? Maybe what happened did not seem funny to you at the time, but as the story is told and retold, you can see the humor in it.

Families and friends have different customs and traditions. Maybe your family enjoys sports events together. Perhaps you and your friend like to go to the movies. We all like to remember happy times. What do you recall about your first day of school? About your last birthday? About a movie you enjoyed?

Photographs keep the past alive. You may have a special photo in your room that reminds you of a good time. When someone at home comes across an old family photograph, perhaps you share it together. Remembering where we have been is important so that we can choose where we want to go.

37

Memories

Maybe some of your important memories are not so happy. Perhaps you were not chosen for a team. Maybe someone did not treat you kindly when you needed it. Or maybe your body was hurt. Some memories bring tears, others bring smiles. Life holds both kinds. Sometimes we appreciate happy memories even more when we have gone through difficult times.

Crucifix (wood sculpture), African

YOUR HISTORY

Write about an event that you recall from your early life.

_____

_____

_____

_____

_____

What event in your life has been kept alive by your family or friends?

_____ .

_____

_____

_____

_____

_____

Jesus meets woman at the well (sculpture), Ivan Mestrovic, University of Notre Dame

38

Emmaus, tapestry detail,
Vatican Museum, Rome, Italy

KEEPING ALIVE THE STORY OF JESUS

Just as you have inherited memories from your family that help you understand your own special story, you have received memories from your Christian family. For centuries, the Church has kept alive the story of Jesus. Christians both retell the story and try to live it.

When Jesus began to teach and heal by the power of God's love, many people came to believe in him. They took his values as their own. They showed in their lives Jesus' call to receive love, healing, and forgiveness, and to offer love to everyone. After his resurrection, Jesus sent the Spirit to help his friends.

The Gospels Make Jesus Present

The first friends of Jesus were excited about the good news of his life, death, and resurrection. The good news is that Jesus came to heal us, to love us, and to teach us to love. The friends of Jesus formed a community in which they might live as Jesus had taught them. They shared with one another what was theirs. They prayed together. They celebrated what Jesus had done for them. They shared with others their memories of Jesus and what he had taught them.

As the years passed, some of the people who had known Jesus went to live in other countries. They shared their memories of him with the people they met. Communities of believers came to be formed in other parts of the world.

For the first twenty or thirty years after Jesus' resurrection, people passed along their memories of Jesus by word of mouth. But how could they be certain that their memories of Jesus would live on after them?

They wanted a lasting account that described who Jesus was and what he had meant to them. They began to put their memories of Jesus in writing. The good news that Jesus had given them would be preserved for everyone. Their writings about Jesus came to be called the gospel. The word *gospel* means "good news."

The gospels still keep alive our memories of Jesus. How is that done? Does the gospel keep our memories alive by retelling what happened almost 2,000 years ago? Or is there something more important than just recalling the past?

The writers of the gospels were **inspired**, or guided in a divine way, by the Holy Spirit. The gospels, like the rest of the Scriptures, are the living word of God. Much more than a retelling of history, the gospels allow the power of God to speak to us in our lives when we read them. As we read the Scriptures, we should pray for the Holy Spirit to guide our understanding.

CALLED BY JESUS

Whom did Jesus first call to follow him? Read the gospel account in Matthew 4:18–22. Then complete these sentences.

In this account, Jesus was walking _____

_____ . He saw two brothers, _____ and

_____ . Jesus said to them, " _____

_____ ."

Read the gospel account in John 1:28, 35–42. Then write in your answers.

Where did this event take place? _____

_____

How many disciples followed Jesus? _____

What did Jesus ask them? _____

_____

How did they answer? _____

_____

What did Andrew say to Jesus? _____

_____

What did Jesus say to Simon? _____

_____

Read John 1:43–51. Write your answers.

Who became disciples of Jesus? _____

What did Nathanael say to Jesus? _____

_____

Read John 4:27–30. Then write your answers.

Who was Jesus talking to? _____

What did she tell her people? _____

_____

The Message of Jesus

Jesus continues to call followers today. You are responding to that invitation by preparing to receive Confirmation.

The gospel accounts of Matthew, Mark, Luke, and John are not alike in every detail. The gospel writers had something more important to tell than just recording historical facts. They wanted to share with others the memories the first Christians had of Jesus so that they could know, admire, and love Jesus as the early Christians had.

What are you to remember of Jesus calling the first disciples? It isn't so much who was called or where. It is the message: Jesus called people to live by his teachings.

The message of Jesus is for all people. However, only some respond. Learning to respond to this message is the work of a lifetime.

In Chapter 4 of John's gospel, we can read the story of a woman who talked with Jesus. Once she knew who he was, she went into town to bring her people to meet him. Many people have followed Jesus because others had told them about him.

To live as a follower of Jesus means that you believe in his message as it is revealed in the Scriptures. The way that God communicates love to us through the Scriptures is called **revelation**. To follow Jesus means that you give witness to this message in your life. Your witness experience and other on-going service you give to others are acts of Christian witness. Your friendliness and loving concern for others can show that you follow Jesus. In the sacraments you find Jesus present in the Church and in your own life.

The liturgy is the Church's public worship of God and public celebration of who Jesus is. We celebrate the Eucharist to honor the Creator in Jesus' name. Jesus is present to us at all times. We remind ourselves of his presence when we call his name in our prayers.

PRESENT IN THE SACRAMENTS

All the sacraments reveal to us the presence of the loving, caring Jesus. Sacraments are living signs through which Jesus touches those who believe in him to strengthen and bless them as they walk with him.

As Jesus once rejoiced with people in their happiness, he rejoices with us today. As Jesus once healed people who were ill, he heals people today. Jesus once comforted people who were troubled; he comforts people today. Jesus once forgave people who had sinned; he forgives people today.

People meet Jesus in a special way in each of the seven sacraments. Each sacrament marks an important moment in people's lives. More than that, Jesus promises to be always present, by the grace of that sacrament, in people's lives. How do you think Jesus is present to people in each of the sacraments?

Sacramental Life

Let us look again at each of the sacraments and their place in your life. Sacraments celebrate and connect our personal stories with our belief in Jesus. The basic, ordinary stuff of life—water, oil, bread, wine—are used in the sacraments to

recall Jesus' presence in our lives. The sacraments are key moments when God's presence celebrates and fills with grace who we are and what we do.

The sacraments of initiation—Baptism, Confirmation, and Eucharist—bring us into new life with God as members of Jesus' Church. In the waters of Baptism, we are reborn and freed from all sin. Through the anointing of Confirmation, we receive anew the gift of the Holy Spirit, who helps us to live as Christians. In the Eucharist, we celebrate the life, death, and resurrection of Jesus; we are nourished by his real presence in the consecrated bread and wine.

Healing and Vocation

The sacraments of **Anointing of the Sick** and **Reconciliation** are often called sacraments of healing. We receive these sacraments at times in our lives when we need to feel the healing presence of Jesus. Through the Anointing of the

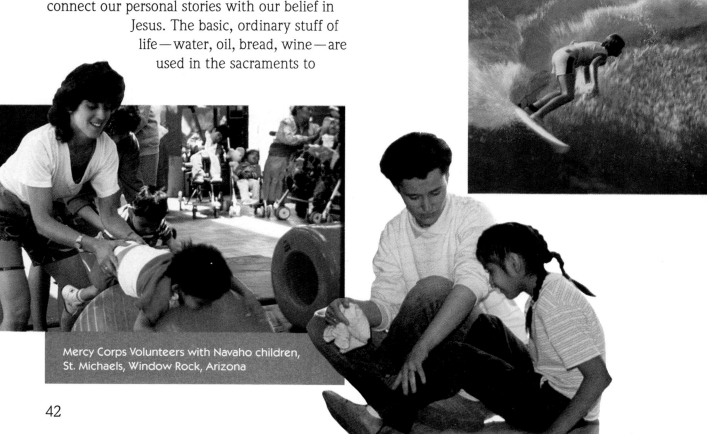

Mercy Corps Volunteers with Navaho children, St. Michaels, Window Rock, Arizona

Sick, people who are ill or elderly are strengthened by Jesus and the Church community. Their faith and hope are renewed.

In the sacrament of Reconciliation, Jesus welcomes us back to our loving and merciful God and to the community of the Church. To receive God's forgiveness in Reconciliation, we must repent of our wrongdoing, be willing to confess the wrongdoing to a priest, make reparation for the wrongdoing, and receive **absolution** from the priest. Through the words of the priest, "I absolve you from your sins in the name of the Father, and of the Son, and of the Holy Spirit," it is Jesus who forgives us.

The sacraments of **Marriage** and **Holy Orders** celebrate two of the choices we might make about the way we live as Christians. In the sacrament of Marriage, a man and a woman become husband and wife through their mutual consent and love. Their love and union become a sign of Jesus' love for the whole Church.

Through Holy Orders, members of the Church community are called to minister as bishops, priests, and deacons. These men are asked to carry on Jesus' caring ministry in a special way. They do this as they lead the Church in celebrating the sacraments, proclaiming the good news, and serving all in need.

IDENTIFYING SACRAMENTS

Write the letter of the correct description by the name of each sacrament.

_____Baptism

_____Confirmation

_____Eucharist

_____Reconciliation

_____Anointing of the Sick

_____Marriage

_____Holy Orders

A. We are welcomed into the Christian community

B. A sacrament in which we receive forgiveness

C. Celebrates the bond of love between a man and a woman

D. Strengthens our commitment to Christ and celebrates the presence of the Spirit

E. Meal in which Christ shares himself with each of us

F. A sacrament that recognizes certain persons for unique service to the Church

G. A sacrament in which we experience the healing presence of Jesus

Tug-of-war, annual Gathering of the Scottish Clans, Grandfather Mountain, North Carolina

PRESENT IN ALL OF LIFE

The sacraments are not the only ways we encounter Jesus. We can see Jesus in people who live the mission he gave to his apostles: to go to all peoples everywhere and make them his disciples (based on Matthew 28:19). Who are the people you know who teach the truths Jesus taught?

Do you know people who try to show the kindness of Jesus to others? You might begin by thinking of your family. Are there some ways in which they show that they care about you, even though they might not say it?

You might think about your friends. Perhaps you have one or two close friends who understand you. You can tell them when something good happens to you, because they will be happy for you. They listen when you want to talk about a problem. They stand by you when you need them. Or perhaps you would like to find these qualities in a friend. Maybe this is the kind of friend you are to another.

What about other people in your life? There might be people who inspire you to live the truth and goodness of Jesus because their lives show his truth and goodness. For example, there might be people who help you grow in knowledge of the word by making a camping trip fun or a scouting experience worthwhile. There might be people who teach skills needed in sports.

There are people you might never meet who visit those who are ill to let them know they have not been forgotten. How about those who work to improve the housing and working conditions of people who need help? Could you ever really name all the ways in which people live the message of Jesus every day?

Sometimes we might not experience enough of the right kind of care from others. At such times Jesus is still present in our lives, loving us. Our faith helps us know this.

Making His Story Your Story

In Confirmation you will choose to say you are a follower of Jesus. There are so many ways to live the love of Jesus—perhaps in the ways that you have received love.

Life is full of surprises; all Jesus asks for is your willingness. He will call you to the ways you might best live his love. "For we are his handiwork, created in Christ Jesus for the good works that God has prepared in advance, that we should live in them" (Ephesians 2:10).

Advocate of the Poor

Ethel Williams is always angry.

"Injustice gets right to my gut—injustice of any kind infuriates me."

At age 66, Ethel Williams is an ardent, outspoken activist for the rights of black people and the poor of all ages, races, and creeds in her inner-city community in Paterson, N.J. Her city ranks in the top ten of the nation's poorest.

Ms. Williams is executive director of the Paterson Diocese Catholic Community Center, which is composed of a thrift shop in the diocese's poorest area and a crisis-intervention center operated out of Williams' own home. Her job takes her wherever a crisis is occurring. "We bury the dead, take care of fire victims—whatever needs to be done," she says.

Ms. Williams keeps a cache of foods donated by suburban parishes, and she parcels it out to those in need. Many donations arrive in response to a newsletter that Ms. Williams publishes. She also speaks to groups and parishes; any stipend earned goes to the center.

In June of 1987, Ms. Williams received a presidential citation from the Presidential Volunteer Action Awards program. In 1986, Ms. Williams became the first black to win the Lumen Christi Award of the Catholic Church Extension Society. Nominated by Paterson Bishop Frank Rodimer, Ms. Williams was lauded for her years of extraordinary service. She had received numerous honors, including the Cross Pro Ecclesia et Pontifice from Pope John Paul II. She says, "Anyone can do what I do, and there are people out there doing it."

Ms. Williams taught public school in Paterson, retiring after 32 years. As a guidance counselor in the 1960s, she became involved with SAGE, a program started by the Paterson school system to encourage pregnant teenagers to continue their high school studies. In her ten years with SAGE, Ms. Williams worked with more than 1,800 teens. Seeing young mothers finish school was a great reward. Her teaching experience has convinced Ms. Williams that education is the only real cure for poverty.

Ms. Williams was one of 10 delegates from Paterson at the National Black Catholic Congress in Washington, D.C.

Ms. Williams founded BLACK (Black Leadership and Catholic Knowledge) which helps black Catholics come together to pray, socialize, and learn from one another.

CELEBRATING: RESPONDING IN FAITH

Leader: Lord, every day in many different ways we are asked to receive your message, to live it, and to share it with others.

Student 1: (Reads from Jeremiah 1:4–8)

Student 2: Lord, help us to hear your call to be your followers.

All: Lord, help us to be your followers.

Student 2: Lord, help us to be your followers and to make no excuses about being too young or too old, too busy or too weak.

All: Lord, help us to be your followers.

Student 2: Lord, help us to respond to your call to each of us. We know you will be present in everything we do.

All: Lord, help us to be your followers.

Student 3: (Reads from Matthew 4:18–22)

Leader: To whom does Jesus say "Come, follow me" today?

Student 2: Lord, you call each of us to follow you.
Help us to understand what that call means.
Help us see our preparation
for the sacrament of Confirmation
as an opportunity to learn how
we might answer your call.
Give each of us the courage
to be recognized as your followers.
We ask this through your Holy Spirit,
who comes to us
as the special gift of Confirmation.

All: Amen.

REVIEWING: RESPONDING IN FAITH

Fill In the Blanks

Sacraments are identified through certain words and signs. Carefully read again the sections on pages 42–43. Then try to identify the following sacraments.

1. The sacrament in which you would hear the words "I absolve you from your sins in the name of the Father, and of the Son, and of the Holy Spirit" is

_____

2. The sacrament in which bread and wine are used is

_____

3. The sacrament in which the Church reaches out to anoint those who are ill is

_____

4. The sacrament that celebrates the love of a man and a woman is

_____

5. The sacrament in which someone would be ordained is

_____

6. The sacraments of initiation are

_____,

_____

_____

7. The sacraments of healing are

_____

and _____.

8. The sacraments that celebrate choices of how we might live our lives are

_____.

and _____.

A Prayer to the Holy Spirit

Write a prayer to the Holy Spirit to guide you in living out the love of Jesus in a special way in your life.

_____

_____

_____

_____

_____

_____

_____

_____

_____

_____

_____

_____

DECLARING OUR BELIEFS

Who do you trust?
Who trusts you?

THINKING ABOUT YOUR BELIEFS

I F someone asked you, "Would you do me a favor?" you might quickly answer yes or no. More likely, you would want to know what the favor was before saying yes or no.

But can you think of someone to whom you might immediately answer yes? This would probably be a person that you know and trust. The way we respond to people has a great deal to do with knowledge and trust. For example, if your best friend were accused of stealing from a locker in school, your first reaction might be to think that the accusation was false because you believe your friend is honest and does not steal.

Our responses are based on our beliefs. And beliefs reveal many things about us. They show the kind of people we are—what we value, our feelings about others, our visions and hopes for the future.

True beliefs take time to develop. That is because beliefs are based on experiences of trust—in other people and in ourselves.

49

BELIEF INVENTORY

Write some of your beliefs.
One thing I believe I do well is

_____ .

One thing I believe about my family is

_____ .

One thing I believe about my best friend is

_____ .

One thing I believe about the world is

_____ .

One thing I believe about people is

_____ .

One thing I hope for the future of the world is

_____ .

CATHOLIC BELIEFS

As we grow and learn, each of us comes to believe certain things about God and our faith.

The early Christians slowly developed their beliefs about God as their understanding grew. Some of the beliefs that some people held were not true, so at various times throughout its history, the pope and bishops of the Church met to clarify beliefs. Statements of belief, called **creeds,** were formulated. These were developed to express our beliefs after many years of careful thought. The creeds were based on the knowledge and trust that the community of the faithful had in God.

One familiar statement of beliefs is the Nicene Creed. We pray this creed at Mass on Sundays and feast days. This profession of faith is from the First Council of Nicaea, held in the year 325. To better appreciate this creed, let us look at each phrase and the meaning of the words we pray.

Mexican workers harvesting aloe, Harlingen, Texas

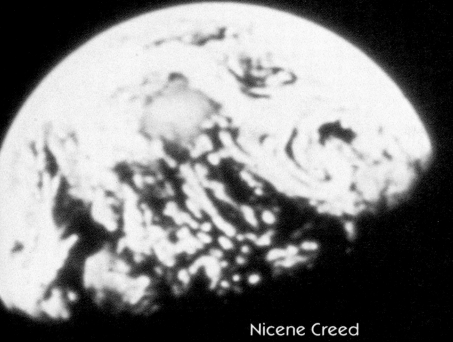

Nicene Creed

We believe in one God,
 the Father, the Almighty,
 maker of heaven and earth,
 of all that is seen and unseen.
We believe in one Lord, Jesus Christ,
 the only Son of God,
 eternally begotten of the Father,
 God from God, Light from Light,
 true God from true God,
 begotten, not made, one in Being with the Father.
 Through him all things were made.
 For us men and for our salvation
  he came down from heaven:
 by the power of the Holy Spirit
  he was born of the Virgin Mary, and became man.
For our sake he was crucified under Pontius Pilate;
 he suffered, died, and was buried.
 On the third day he rose again
  in fulfillment of the Scriptures;
 he ascended into heaven
  and is seated at the right hand of the Father.
He will come again in glory to judge the living and the dead,
 and his kingdom will have no end.
We believe in the Holy Spirit, the Lord, the giver of life,
 who proceeds from the Father and the Son.
 With the Father and the Son he is worshiped and glorified.
 He has spoken through the Prophets.
 We believe in one holy catholic and apostolic Church.
 We acknowledge one baptism for the forgiveness of sins.
 We look for the resurrection of the dead,
  and the life of the world to come. Amen.

Village children sharing rice meal,
Dacca, Bangladesh

The Nicene Creed
We
We belong to the family of God. At Mass, we join in the family prayer. Our faith is made stronger when we share it with our community.

believe in one God,
Together we are the Church. There are many things in our lives that we are happy about. There are many things about our world that we do not understand and many things we would like to change. We struggle to trust and have faith.

the Father,
God creates each of us out of love and continues to look after us.

the Almighty,
God is good, the source of life. God has a special, loving plan for each of us. Our challenge is to live so that this plan is revealed.

maker of heaven and earth,
God made a beautiful universe and wants us to share it in happiness with God and with one another. God gives meaning to life. When life as we know it ends, God calls us to greater joy.

of all that is seen and unseen.
God is Creator; all things have their beginning in God's love.

We believe in one Lord, Jesus Christ,
Through Jesus Christ, the divine love for us was revealed in all its greatness.

the only Son of God,
In faith we believe that God is revealed to us in Jesus. We believe that, through Jesus, God is present in every created thing.

eternally begotten of the Father,
Jesus is the Word of God. He comes to speak to us of God's love, love that is always with us in all that we do.

God from God, Light from Light, true God from true God,
Jesus reveals to us that we share life with God. As we commit ourselves to Jesus, he shows us the love within all of life. Our faith in Jesus helps us try to make this world a more loving place.

begotten, not made, one in Being with the Father.
When God gave us Jesus, he was giving us his Word, his love, his life. God gives us his own self.

Through him all things were made.
Jesus shows us that God is Creator and Redeemer as Jesus guides our lives.

For us men and for our salvation he came down from heaven:
Jesus came to bring us God's love and care and to show us how to love and care for ourselves and one another.

by the power of the Holy Spirit
God makes us God's family. God becomes one of us through Jesus.

he was born of the Virgin Mary, and became man.
God's plan was carried out because of a young girl named Mary. She is the mother of Jesus Christ, the Son of God.

For our sake he was crucified under Pontius Pilate; he suffered, died, and was buried.
Jesus' love for people, his teaching, and the way he lived were so unusual that political leaders feared him and put him to death. His life and even his death were, for us, signs of God's love.

On the third day he rose again
By raising Jesus, God shows us how loved we are and that our life with God will never end. We believe that Jesus is always present with us.

in fulfillment of the Scriptures;
In the resurrection, God made true the hopes of the written word. Belief in the risen Jesus, and in our own eternal life, was the proof of love on which the Church community began.

he ascended into heaven
and is seated at the right hand of the Father.
All that is good comes from God and becomes one with God. We pray to the Father through Jesus.

He will come again in glory to judge the living and the dead,
Jesus is with us in the gospels, in the Church, and in the sacraments. Jesus' gospel of love will be the measure of how well we have lived.

and his kingdom will have no end.
Finally and forever there will be peace and justice, and we will love one another.

We believe in the Holy Spirit, the Lord, the giver of life,
Love between people sometimes seems so vivid that there is a living spirit that binds us together. It is the Spirit of God's love that gives new life.

who proceeds from the Father and the Son.
This Holy Spirit is God's very life and love given to us through Jesus. The Holy Spirit empowers each person with special gifts to live in faith and give witness to Jesus Christ.

Anniversary Civil Rights March on Washington, D.C.

With the Father and the Son he is worshiped and glorified.
We believe in one God. The Spirit is vital and alive and dwells in us to enable us to know, love, and praise God.

He has spoken through the prophets.
Through the Spirit, God has in many different ways shared life and love, guiding us to action.

We believe in one holy catholic and apostolic Church.
Today, the Spirit speaks through members of the Church. Our Church prays to be united in belief, to be full of goodness, to be faithful to Jesus' gospel, and to bring it to all people.

We acknowledge one baptism for the forgiveness of sins.
Jesus said, "Go, therefore, and make disciples of all nations, baptizing them in the name of the Father, and of the Son, and of the holy Spirit" (Matthew 28:19). This is the basis for our Baptism as Christians: we are welcomed into the family of Jesus, we are offered forgiveness, and we are called to share in new life.

We look for the resurrection of the dead, and the life of the world to come. Amen.
Jesus brought to fulfillment his teaching that the dead would be raised to new life. He said that God "is not the God of the dead but of the living" (Matthew 22:32). We believe we will share in the glorified life of Jesus. We believe in God, who is life and love, and in Jesus and the Spirit, who reveal truth and help us follow the way of love. We look forward to joy with God and one another forever.

Professing Our Beliefs

In the sacrament of Confirmation, the Holy Spirit calls us to give public witness to what we believe as Catholic Christians. We declare by our actions and our attitudes that we are followers of Jesus and members of his Church.

During the ceremony, all who are to be confirmed will stand before God, the bishop, and the people of your parish. Together you will profess faith in God the Father; in Jesus Christ, God's only Son, our Lord; in the Holy Spirit, the giver of life; and in the holy Catholic Church.

The bishop will confirm the profession of faith with these words: **This is our faith. This is the faith of the Church. We are proud to profess it in Christ Jesus our Lord.**

As we choose to follow Jesus, we accept the attitudes of Jesus. His entire message was one of compassionate love and mercy, of actions of peace for the good of people.

Inset: Traditional face make-up, Calcutta, India
Above: Native dancer, annual Gueleguetza gathering, Oaxaca, Mexico

Celebration for the elderly, Cincinnati, Ohio

A MESSAGE OF COMPASSION

Read Luke 10:25–37. Then answer
the questions.
Write the commandment that Jesus tells us is
the greatest.

_____

_____

What parable did Jesus tell to describe who our

neighbor is? _____

Describe a way you could live this parable today.

THE BEATITUDES

The **Beatitudes** of Jesus give us ways to live the
great commandment. People who try to live by
this "way of the blessed" open their minds and
hearts to the call of God and the needs of others.
When we ourselves are in need, we try to have
faith and trust that God will reach us through
the care of others.

Blessed are the poor in spirit,
   for theirs is the kingdom of heaven.
Blessed are they who mourn,
   for they will be comforted.
Blessed are the meek,
   for they will inherit the land.
Blessed are they who hunger and thirst for
      righteousness,
   for they will be satisfied.
Blessed are the merciful,
   for they will be shown mercy.
Blessed are the clean of heart,
   for they will see God.
Blessed are the peacemakers,
   for they will be called children of God.
Blessed are they who are persecuted for the
      sake of righteousness,
   for theirs is the kingdom of heaven.
Blessed are you when they insult you and
persecute you and utter every kind of
evil against you [falsely] because of me.
Rejoice and be glad, for your reward will
be great in heaven. Thus they persecuted
the prophets who were before you.
Matthew 5:3–12

Living the Beatitudes

To be **poor in spirit** is to look to God for our fulfillment. We trust that God wants us to be happy. We believe that caring for the needs of others can bring happiness. The poor in spirit make their plans like everyone else. They look forward to a good life. When difficulties come, such as a death, the loss of a job, the birth of a sick child, they can adapt because they are open to what life brings.

Those who **mourn** are people who are not deadened to the pain of others. Perhaps after watching a TV show about hunger, or a segment of the news, they might mourn for the suffering of others. They know we are all united. We have compassion for those who suffer. We trust that God looks after suffering people. We seek ways to bring joy where there is sadness.

The **meek** treat all people with dignity. They are not falsely humble, claiming that they are not talented, nor do they let people walk all over them. They know that the gifts they have been given—their intelligence, humor, and skills—are things they can share with others.

The meek regard all life as a gift and seek to use God's gifts in life-giving ways. By their gentle presence, they seek to bring peace and freedom. In their gentleness there is great strength.

Those who **hunger and thirst for righteousness** seek to know and carry out God's plan for all people. They work to correct injustice so that everyone can share in God's gifts. They care enough to be involved in significant causes.

The **merciful** care about the needs of others. They do not judge others but try to forgive and offer help when it is needed. The merciful live by the golden rule. They treat others as they would like to be treated.

The **clean of heart** live simply. Loving God is foremost in their lives. They care more about loving others than about owning many things. They share themselves with others and, in the sharing, discover God.

The **peacemakers** work to guarantee human rights for all people. They bring God's peace by opposing violence with peaceful actions.

Those who are **persecuted for the sake of righteousness** are people who live a good, honest life. They don't stop doing what they know is right, even though they might be punished for their work. They trust that God's love can bring good out of evil.

Jesus taught that acting on our belief in God can be difficult; if we do the right thing, we can expect to be criticized. The values expressed by the Beatitudes seem to run counter to many of the values found in today's society. Living as "Beatitude people" is our most profound challenge as Christians. In Theme Six we will explore how the Holy Spirit helps us meet this challenge.

Ministering in Palau

As Act One of the Passion play opened, Chris Banks looked on from behind the scenes, from the sacristy of a small church in Palau, an island group in the Pacific Ocean. He had worked long, hard hours with the boys and girls of the youth group. The youth were from the local public and mission schools. Chris regarded the Passion play as an entertaining way to educate the boys and girls and help them create a unique Holy Week experience for the people of the parish.

Chris grew up in a large family, the youngest of ten children. His father died when Chris was 14. His mother worked hard to support the family and keep them together. Chris was always willing to help in any way that he could. He was an active member of his parish youth group.

While in high school, he helped with a special Holy Week project sponsored by the diocese that provided service to people in need. The youth cleaned up an inner-city tenement building, painting, scrubbing, and making it a pleasant place to live. In a nursing home, they scrubbed floors and cleaned the grounds. Each evening, exhausted, they ended with the liturgy of the day. They experienced what the message of service meant in their lives.

Chris came to see Holy Week as an opportunity to provide special service. He was a leader both in his parish and in the diocese. He encouraged the members of the Confirmation class each year to become members of the youth group. He was a force behind the parish's decision to hire a youth minister; he spoke for the youth to the parish council.

Chris was a parish eucharistic minister. He attended the University of Scranton in Pennsylvania. As the time for graduation drew near, Chris heard a plea for volunteers from the Jesuit International Volunteers. Chris felt drawn to their work. Chris thought about the gifts in his life. He believed that these gifts were given for the good of all to be shared. Was two years of his life too much to ask? Could he respond to the call?

Chris' mother was not really surprised to hear of his new plan. Now each letter that arrives from Chris tells of new projects and new ways he has found to teach the children.

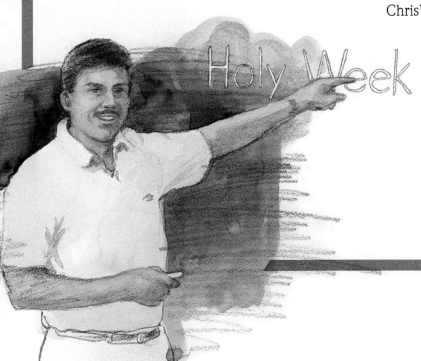

Holy Week

CELEBRATING: DECLARING OUR BELIEFS

Leader: Lord, we know that we are called to be your followers, but how can we serve you? You have said to us "For I was hungry and you gave me food; I was thirsty and you gave me drink."

All: Lord, when did we see you hungry and feed you or see you thirsty and give you drink?

Leader: "I was a stranger and you welcomed me, naked and you clothed me."

All: Lord, when did we welcome you away from home or clothe you?

Leader: "I was ill and you comforted me, in prison and you came to visit me."

All: Lord, when did we visit you when you were ill or in prison?

Leader: "As often as you did it for one of my brothers or sisters, you did it for me."

Adapted from Matthew 25:31—46

Student 1: (Reads from Matthew 5:13–16)

All: God our Father,
We believe in you.
We believe in Jesus.
We believe in the Holy Spirit.
Our belief leads us beyond ourselves.
We want to take our beliefs seriously.
We want to accept the responsibilities of a Christian.
We pray for your help through your Son and the Holy Spirit.

Student 2: **God our Father,**
complete the work you have begun
and keep the gifts of your Holy Spirit
active in the hearts of your people.
Make them ready to live his Gospel
and eager to do his will.
May they never be ashamed
to proclaim to all the world Christ crucified
living and reigning for ever and ever.

All: **Amen.**

REVIEWING: DECLARING OUR BELIEFS

Beatitude People

Read each story below. From the list of beatitudes, choose one or two to go with each story. Then write an ending for each story based upon the beatitude you chose. You may use a beatitude more than once.

is poor in spirit	hungers and thirsts for righteousness	mourns
is clean of heart	is persecuted for the sake of righteousness	is meek
is a peacemaker		

George is clever on the school computer. He is saving to buy a computer of his own. He tutors younger students. One boy is doing well because George spends extra time with him. But George could work with another student and earn more.

_____

_____

_____

Jean's mom tells her she and dad are getting divorced. Jean will live with her mom. Jean is sad over the loss. Her mom wants to talk with her about their plans for their new life.

_____

_____

_____

Peter knows that his friend is jealous because he was chosen to play snare drums in the school band. Peter wants to accept the offer, but he doesn't want his friend to be mad at him.

_____

_____

_____

Erin is captain of the basketball team. Going to practice every day is hard work. Gina likes to go to parties and stay out late. The next day she doesn't play as well. Yesterday she missed a shot that cost the team the game.

_____

_____

_____

Carlos has been out of school for three weeks recovering from an injury. His teacher asks if someone would help him catch up in math.

_____

_____

After the game, the team likes to go to Charlie's house to make sandwiches. Charlie asks them to clean up and not leave a mess for his mom. Some of the boys laugh at Charlie and tell him to clean up because it is his house.

_____

_____

THE GIFTS OF THE SPIRIT

If you were to display one of your talents, which one might it be?

TALENTS AND GIFTS

EVERYONE has talents, with unique ways of using them. Some talents are natural abilities. We learn to develop other talents as we grow as Christians and as human beings.

Do you know what your special talents are? You might be a good listener or perhaps you're great on the guitar. When we use our talents, they grow stronger.

As we attempt to grow in the Christian life, spiritual gifts that we received in Baptism help us to grow. In Baptism, the Holy Spirit gave us the gift of new life, the new life of faith. The Holy Spirit brought us God's love and peace.

We Live Our Beliefs

In Confirmation the Spirit renews God's power within us. We describe this power as the **seven gifts of the Spirit.** These gifts help us to know the best way to live as Christians, and they give us the strength to do so. These gifts are described in Isaiah 11:1–9.

In the rite of Confirmation the bishop will pray that the Holy Spirit will help us live as followers of Jesus:

> **All-powerful God, Father of our Lord Jesus Christ,**
> **by water and the Holy Spirit**
> **you freed your sons and daughters from sin**
> **and gave them new life.**
> **Send your Holy Spirit upon them**
> **to be their Helper and Guide.**
> **Give them the spirit of wisdom and understanding,**
> **the spirit of right judgment and courage,**
> **the spirit of knowledge and reverence.**
> **Fill them with the spirit of wonder and awe in your presence.**
> **We ask this through Christ our Lord.**

GIFTS OF THE SPIRIT

The Holy Spirit helps us as we try to grow in all the good moral qualities by which a person becomes great. The gifts of the Holy Spirit all proceed from God's love. The gifts work together.

The gift of **wisdom** helps us look upon life as a great and remarkable gift from God. Wisdom helps us recognize God's presence in all people, places, and things. Wisdom helps us judge events in our lives according to our belief in God. For example, a physical therapist is given grace to love the disabled children she works with.

The gift of **understanding** leads us beyond just knowing the beliefs of the Church. We grasp the meaning of what we believe and act in ways that show our Christian faith makes a difference. Understanding and faith grow together. It helps us discover God's plan in our lives. It helps us touch the lives of others in service. A teacher who is patient with the varying abilities of children exemplifies understanding.

The gift of **knowledge** helps us to be certain that God cares for us. It calls us to live a life of loving actions wherever we are—at home, in school, on the basketball court, at the mall, with friends. Knowledge shows us how the truths of our faith give direction to our lives. We come together to share our faith. For example, a coach who helps his team "hang in" and do their best even when they have a losing season knows it is important to teach good sportsmanship.

The gift of **right judgment** helps us see right and good things to do among the many choices we have to make every day. It helps us choose the right way to act. It helps us to guide others and to seek the guidance of others when we need it. The girl who chooses not to join her friends when they drink beer at a party shows right judgment.

The gift of **courage** helps us to be strong in our beliefs as Christians. It helps us choose what is right in spite of any hardship we might suffer. As we act in courage, our faith and hope in God grow stronger. Courage helps us make our world a better place for all people. For example, the man who spends weekends helping homeless people find temporary housing even though his co-workers ridicule him shows courage.

The gift of **reverence** helps us honor God as most loving Creator and all people as our brothers and sisters. It encourages us to praise God freely and grows as we pray. This gift helps us choose to act peacefully in love. For example, the boy who is kind to the classmate whom other boys tease shows reverence.

The gift of **wonder and awe** in God's presence helps us respect the goodness and majesty of God. It helps us to value God's plan for the world and to desire to build up the kingdom of God on earth. We treasure all of God's creation because it conveys God's love. Wonder and awe help us to be grateful to God for the gift of life and encourage us to worship God. For example, the teens who help out with the town's recycling by delivering collection buckets show respect for the gifts of creation.

Helping out in Appalachia

LIVING THE GIFTS

Think of people you know who show one or more gifts of the Spirit. Write the names of the persons and the gifts on the lines.

_____

_____

_____

Give examples of occasions when these persons have used these gifts.

_____

_____

_____

Prayer over the People

At the end of the Confirmation ceremony, the bishop will pray that we may live the gospel as faithful witnesses to Jesus Christ. He will pray:

**God our Father,
complete the work you have begun
and keep the gifts of your Holy Spirit
active in the hearts of your people.
Make them ready to live his Gospel
and eager to do his will.
May they never be ashamed
to proclaim to all the world Christ
crucified
living and reigning for ever and ever.**

Together with all present you will answer, "Amen." By your Amen you will be saying, "Yes, I want to be responsible to others and to the Church. The Church has kept for me the message of the gospel, the history of a believing community, and the sacraments. I can respond to this inheritance."

63

A Look Back

You are completing your preparation for the sacrament of Confirmation. When you began, you signed an Enrollment Promise. You agreed to do what was asked of you.

Since you signed that promise, you have attended learning sessions and have shared in prayer celebrations. You have also worked on a witness experience. Those activities have helped you understand what Confirmation is.

WHAT CONFIRMATION MEANS FOR YOU

What facts have you learned about the sacrament of Confirmation that are most important to you?

_____

_____

_____

What did you experience at the celebrations that meant a lot to you?

_____

_____

_____

What did you learn from doing your service project?

_____

_____

_____

Understanding Confirmation

We can more fully understand Confirmation if we understand the Church. The sacraments of Baptism, Confirmation, and Eucharist initiate us into the life of the Church. We are invited to become more like Christ in all we do.

You were probably so young when you were baptized that the event has to be recalled for you. You can remember your first reception of the Eucharist. You were probably about seven or eight years old.

Your Confirmation looks back to your Baptism and allows you to say yes to what was done for you. Your Confirmation also looks ahead to how you can build your faith through the use of the gifts of the Spirit and the celebration of the Eucharist.

Baptism and Confirmation are celebrated once in your lifetime. The Eucharist is the ongoing sign of your membership in the Church. What does the Catholic Church mean to you? When you think about the Church, do you think about a community, an organization, or something else?

The Church is an organization, but it is more. The Church is people—the People of God—who share faith in Jesus as Lord. It is people who try to live the gospel message every day.

Celebration of consecration of Bishop Ramirez, San Antonio, Texas

The Church Is . . .

The Church is the Body of Christ. "Now you are Christ's body, and individually parts of it" (1 Corinthians 12:27). Each follower of Jesus has a unique role to play. Whether one is a student, a teacher, a business person, a priest, a counselor, a construction worker, a mother—he or she can serve others in the name of Jesus.

The Bible describes the Church in various ways. One is of a shepherd and his flock. Jesus is the good shepherd. His people are his flock. In nature, sheep are very obedient and follow the shepherd. Read John 10:14, 15.

The Church is called a vineyard. Jesus is the vine; we are branches. Read John 15:4. Paul compared the Church to a building with Jesus as its foundation. Read the verses in 1 Corinthians 3:9, 11.

YOUR PARISH STORY

Fill in the blanks below with the proper names. You are a Catholic Christian. You became a member of the Catholic Church at Baptism.

You are a member of _____ parish.

The bishop of the diocese is _____ . He or one of his associate bishops will come to your parish when you celebrate the sacrament of Confirmation. The pastor of your parish is

_____ .

Many people serve in your parish. Some have chosen to serve in the various ministries as their full-time occupation. Others choose to volunteer some of their time. Learn about the various ways that people serve in your parish.

Volunteer Service

Many other people, possibly among them your parents or a relative, serve the parish as volunteers. Perhaps you are an altar server or a teacher's aid in a parish religious education class. Your parish might have a parish council on which people serve. People also serve as lectors and eucharistic ministers at the liturgy.

Some people volunteer to teach in the religious education program. Your Confirmation teacher may be one of these people. Your parish might have a team that instructs and welcomes adults who are joining the Church through the Rites of Christian Initiation of Adults (R.C.I.A.). Perhaps your parish sponsors a youth group that is directed by adults.

People in your parish may volunteer their services in outreach projects, that is, in helping others who may or may not be in the parish. Such activities might include helping with a food pantry, day care help for mothers of young children, and clothing recycling projects. Perhaps some people visit those who are shut-in because of illness, age, or disability, or use their skills to help in job-training programs for people with special needs.

The Pope's Role

A group of neighboring parishes make up a diocese and are united under the care of a bishop. Dioceses are united to the pope through faith. The pope is the visible head of the Church. He is the successor of Peter. Together with the bishops of the world, he teaches and cares for the needs of the Church throughout the world.

In his teachings, the pope has the same authority that Peter had. When the pope and his bishops encourage people to live in faith and love, they are showing Jesus' care for all people. They are living out the words of Jesus to his disciples, "Go, therefore, and make disciples of all nations" (Matthew 28:19).

Spirit in Your Life

Confirmation celebrates the presence of the Spirit in our lives. This presence of the Spirit has been part of the Church's understanding from the beginning. In John 14:15—21 Jesus promises he will not leave his friends as orphans. He will send the Holy Spirit to help us know the truth that Jesus is always with us.

Signs of the Spirit

From the beginning, the Church has seen the gift of the Holy Spirit as that which sets us apart. This gift of the Creator is the life source Jesus left with the Church after his resurrection. In Paul's letter to the Galatians, he told us how our lives can be signs that point to the presence of the Spirit for ourselves and others.

As we use the gifts of the Spirit, our lives show certain qualities we call virtues. As we live these virtues, they are strengthened in us.

VIRTUES OF THE SPIRIT

Read Galatians 5:22. List below the virtues that Paul points out as **signs of the Spirit.**

_____

_____

_____

_____

_____

_____

_____

_____

Strengthening Your Membership

Now is the time to ask yourself some questions. Do you want to affirm your faith in Jesus and in his Church through Confirmation? Are you ready to stand before the people of your parish and say yes to your faith as a Catholic? Only you can decide.

WHAT YOU DECIDE

Write your answers on the lines below. What is your decision about asking for the sacrament of Confirmation?

_____

_____

_____

_____

Asking for Confirmation

Do you want to affirm in public your belief in Jesus Christ and his Church? If so, you might formally ask to receive the sacrament of Confirmation. Since the bishop celebrates Confirmation, he is the one you should ask.

You should explain why you want to be confirmed. Describe how you have prepared to receive the sacrament. Name the person or persons you have chosen to present you to the bishop in the Confirmation ceremony. State the name you wish to be called at your Confirmation and the reason for your choice. Finally, you should tell how you hope to live the gifts of the Spirit as a member of your parish and a follower of Jesus everywhere you go.

JUST THE BEGINNING

You are completing your formal preparation for Confirmation. One day this book will be a keepsake of your preparation. From time to time you might want to refer to it to refresh your memory as you grow in the gifts of the Spirit.

Has your preparation for Confirmation changed your ideas about the Church? Have you come to a new understanding of Confirmation? How do you see yourself as a member of the Church?

Write your answers in the lines below.
How has your preparation helped you to pray and take part in the life of your parish?

_____

_____

_____

_____

_____

_____

_____

In Confirmation you accept a more responsible role in the Church. You are called to an attitude of service both in the Church and in other aspects of your life. Perhaps in the future you may choose to serve the Church as a layperson, a vowed religious, or an ordained priest or deacon. To be a member means to be involved. Reflect on what that means for you.

Receiving Confirmation is your pledge to witness to Christ every day, wherever you are, whatever you do.

Witness

Helping in the Parish

Frank Roth and his wife, Audrey, were having breakfast when the phone rang. As soon as he heard the voice of Anne, the parish secretary, Frank knew that someone was in need.

Frank can fix just about anything; that's how he first got involved in the church when he and Audrey moved to Florida 15 years ago. Frank, now 79 years old, moved there after he retired as a railroad executive.

One Sunday he noticed several little things that needed repair in the church. Frank volunteered to do those jobs and before long he was called upon almost daily. From fixing lights or the copying machine, he moved to helping meet the more essential human needs. He became a member of the Saint Vincent de Paul Society, a group dedicated to reaching out to people in need.

Members of the Saint Vincent de Paul Society consider each need and how help can be provided. Sometimes the need is for food, other times for money or even for a job. This morning's caller needed all three.

Anne related a story of a family in need. The father had been in the hospital. The mother had lost her job because she had been absent from work too often, trying to care for her family. They were in need of both food and rent assistance.

Frank went down to the parish house to prepare bags of food from the pantry stocked by the Society members. He had a check made out for the rent. He made phone calls and came up with a possibility for part-time employment for the mother.

After leaving the rectory, Frank picked up another member of the Society, and they delivered the food, paid the rent, and told the mother about the job opportunity. She was very grateful. They shared prayer; the mother had been given the financial means and the supportive encouragement she needed to make it through another few weeks. Frank believes the Lord has blessed him; he loves to return those blessings in service.

CELEBRATING: THE GIFTS OF THE SPIRIT

All: Lord, you call us to confirm our membership in the Catholic Church and to openly profess our faith in you. We ask for your help as we try to live out that commitment to you. We pray through your Holy Spirit, who will come to us in a new way in the sacrament of Confirmation.

Student 1: (Reads from Acts 2:1–4.)

Student 2: Lord, teach us to be your followers.

All: Send your Holy Spirit to us.

Student 2: Lord, help us to sing your praise in our hearts and in our deeds.

All: Send your Holy Spirit to us.

Student 2: Lord, heal the sick, comfort the sad and tired, help us to build a world of justice and peace.

All: Send your Holy Spirit to us.

Leader: **All-powerful God, Father of our Lord Jesus Christ,
by water and the Holy Spirit
you freed your sons and daughters from sin
and gave them new life.
Send your Holy Spirit upon them
to be their Helper and Guide.
Give them the spirit of wisdom and understanding,
the spirit of right judgment and courage,
the spirit of knowledge and reverence.
Fill them with the spirit of wonder and awe in your
presence.
We ask this through Christ our Lord.**

All: **Amen.**

REVIEWING: THE GIFTS OF THE SPIRIT

Choosing Gifts

Read each story below. From the list of the gifts of the Spirit, choose a gift to go with each story. Then write an ending for each story.

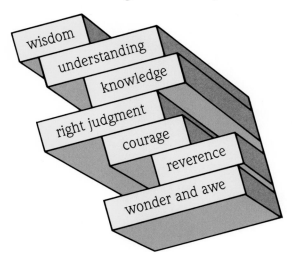

wisdom
understanding
knowledge
right judgment
courage
reverence
wonder and awe

Alison hasn't been doing very well in school. Each quarter her grades seem to slip more. She has a test this morning. Her dad had just left for a short business trip. Alison thinks of skipping school.

_____

_____

_____

Joan and Maria like to play in the waves and look for shells at the beach. One day they noticed a sign that invited people to help keep the beach clean. So this time they have brought big trash bags.

_____

_____

_____

Peter's religion teacher asked if some students would like to help with the first-grade class. If the first-grade teacher has some helpers, she can do extra activities with the children. Peter likes little kids.

_____

_____

_____

When Carla gets ready for bed, she likes to spend a few minutes thinking about the events of her day. She thanks God for the good things that happened. She asks God to help her grow from the things that happened that weren't so nice.

_____

_____

_____

Terry's grandmother has difficulty walking so she doesn't go out too much anymore. She looks forward to Terry's visits. She likes to tell Terry stories of her own school days. She also likes to hear about the kind of music Terry likes and her activities.

_____

_____

_____

Living by God's Word

Living by God's Word

OUR JOURNEY BEGINS

Living the Christian life is often compared to being on a journey. As we try to follow Jesus, we don't know exactly where our lives will take us, but we do know that God is always with us. Jesus wants us to carry on the work that he did. In the gospels, we can read how Jesus sent his disciples out to continue his work.

In your Bible, look up the verses, Luke 9:1–6. Read them thoughtfully a few times. Ask God to help you understand this passage. Then answer the following questions.

What did Jesus give his twelve apostles?

_____

_____

_____

What did Jesus tell his apostles to take with them?

_____

_____

_____

Why, do you think, did Jesus say that?

_____

_____

_____

_____

_____

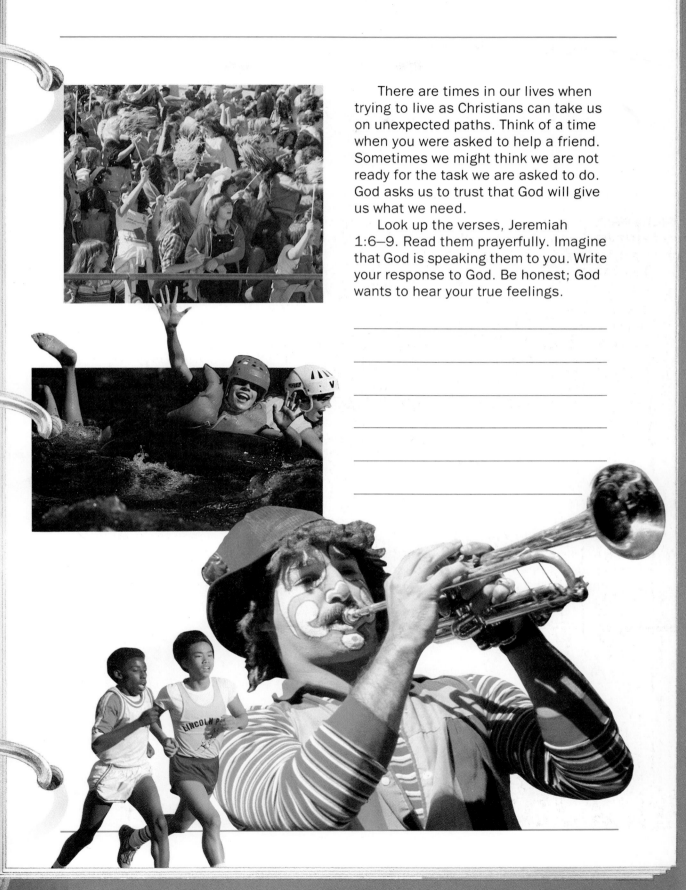

There are times in our lives when trying to live as Christians can take us on unexpected paths. Think of a time when you were asked to help a friend. Sometimes we might think we are not ready for the task we are asked to do. God asks us to trust that God will give us what we need.

Look up the verses, Jeremiah 1:6—9. Read them prayerfully. Imagine that God is speaking them to you. Write your response to God. Be honest; God wants to hear your true feelings.

_____

_____

_____

_____

_____

_____

Living by God's Word

GROWING AS CHRISTIANS

As we use the gifts of the Spirit, our lives show certain qualities we call virtues. As we live these virtues, they grow stronger in us. "A good person out of the store of goodness in his heart produces good . . ." (Luke 6:45).

In this section, you will have an opportunity to explore one or more of the virtues of the Holy Spirit—love, joy, peace, patience, kindness, generosity, gentleness, faithfulness, and self-control.

One of the virtues we seek in our lives is love.

LOVE

Love is creative power that helps people grow the way God intends. Sometimes growing seems easy; often growth comes with pain. When we are loving, we act in kindness toward others, even those who seem difficult to love. We regard all people as worthy of love and understanding, including ourselves.

Jesus tells us, "You shall love your neighbor as yourself" (Matthew 22:39). For some of us, it is easier to love others than to love ourselves. Sometimes we judge ourselves too harshly. We need to regard ourselves with love by standing up for our rights to be protected, respected, and cared for.

Love is not just a feeling; it is a decision to act in a particular way. We *choose* to spend time listening to another, looking for the good qualities in another. We *choose* to be welcoming and to be happy at another's success. Love sometimes means choosing to do the difficult, even when we do not feel like it. It might mean choosing not to retaliate when someone has hurt us.

In 1 Corinthians 13:4—7, we find a description of love. Look this up. Read it a few times. Write some qualities of love named in these verses.

_____

_____

_____

_____

_____

_____

Think of someone in your life who has taught you about love by the way he or she has acted toward you. Explain how this person's example helped you to learn some of these qualities.

_____

_____

_____

_____

_____

Living by God's Word

WITNESSING TO JESUS

The Holy Spirit helps us experience in our lives the virtue of joy.

JOY

To live in Christian joy is to look for God's grace in each situation, even in difficult times when there seems no reason for joy. Joy comes from trusting that God cares for us and gives us the strength we need to overcome troubles. Joy comes from knowing that problems can be pathways to growth. Christian joy comes from helping others discover this in our care for them.

As we are thankful for God's plan in our lives, our ability to express joy becomes stronger. We place our hope in God's plan that makes "all things work for good for those who love God, who are called according to his purpose" (Romans 8:28).

In Paul's first letter to the Thessalonians, he refers to his struggles to bring the gospel message to people. He praises the people of Thessalonica for following his example. In your Bible, look up 1 Thessalonians 1:5—6. Read the verses a few times, asking God to help you understand them.

Think about a time when you experienced joy after doing something that was difficult. What did you have to do? How was it resolved? How did you feel afterward? Would you do it the same way again? Write about your experience.

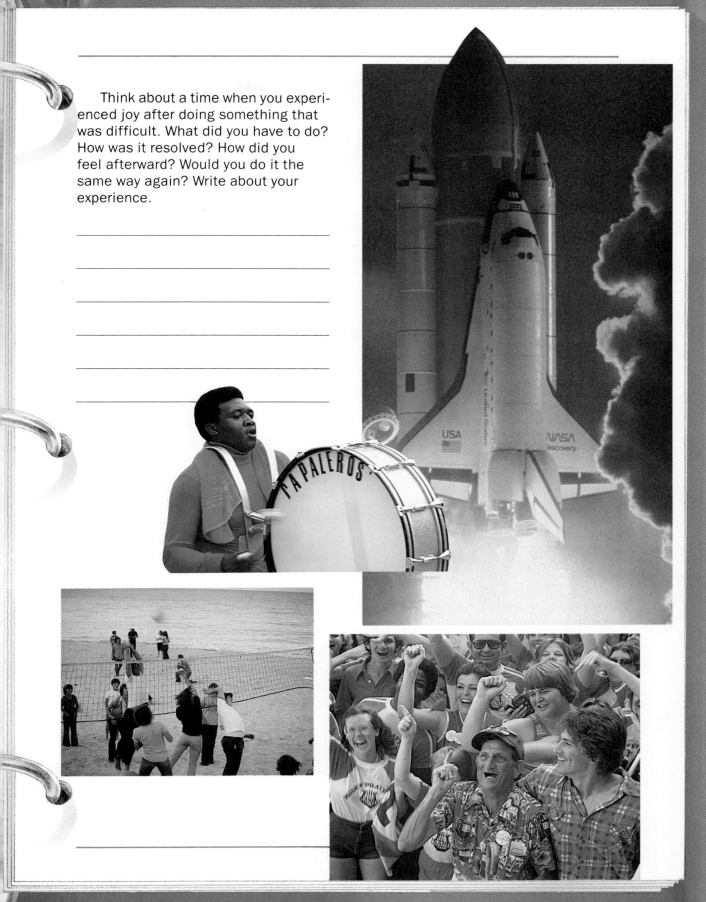

Living by God's Word

RESPONDING IN FAITH

The virtues of peace and patience show the presence of the Holy Spirit in our lives.

PEACE

After his resurrection, Jesus greeted his fearful disciples with the words, "Peace be with you" (John 20:19). Christian peace comes from trusting that God's love is always with us, making all things work together for the good. God's peace helps us to be reconciled with each other.

Peace and justice work together. Often we must work hard to bring peace into a situation. Christians work to help end war and to change conditions that deprive people of their human rights.

In situations of conflict, such as arguments among friends, we can help bring about peaceful reconciliation.

In the gospel of John, at the last supper, Jesus tells his apostles that when he is no longer with them in a visible way, he will send the Holy Spirit to be with them. Another name for the Holy Spirit is the Advocate, or Helper.

In your Bible, read the verses in John 14:25—27. Then answer the following questions.

In whose name will the Father send the Holy Spirit?

_____

What do you think Jesus means when he says, "Not as the world gives do I give it to you" (John 14:27)?

_____

_____

_____

PATIENCE

Christian patience helps us to understand that each person is unique and has different strengths and limitations. It is true of God's ongoing creation that not one of us is "finished." We continually grow and change.

Patience means never giving up hope that we and others can improve, yet being tolerant when change seems slow to come. Patience is merciful support that keeps on hoping.

Paul, in his letter to the Romans, describes the ways Christians should be with one another. In your Bible, look up Romans 15:1—5. Read the verses thoughtfully and prayerfully.

Think of some way in which you are impatient with yourself. How could you be more patient?

_____

_____

_____

Think of someone in your family or at school who needs you to be more patient. Explain how you might improve.

_____

_____

_____

DECLARING OUR BELIEFS

Our actions can show the virtues of kindness, generosity, and gentleness working together when the Holy Spirit is active in our lives.

KINDNESS

Kindness is love in action, an attitude of mercy toward others. To act in kindness is to act as Jesus did, in caring service. Our kindness to another, even someone who does not value it, provides the other with an opportunity to meet God. "The kindness of God would lead you to repentance . . ." (Romans 2:4).

GENEROSITY

To be generous is to do good without measuring the cost. It is to regard others without judgment, to be ready to forgive those who hurt us. We trust that God will provide us with ways to get what we need. "Give and gifts will be given to you; a good measure, packed together, shaken down, and overflowing, will be poured into your lap" (Luke 6:38).

GENTLENESS

We are called to be gentle in our manner with others even when those around us see gentleness as a sign of weakness. We are gentle because God is gentle with us. Being gentle can be a sign of strength. Gentleness works with kindness and patience to help others grow. Jesus treated people gently. "A bruised reed he will not break, a smoldering wick he will not quench . . ." (Matthew 12:20).

Read the story of the anointing of Jesus as told in Mark's gospel, Mark 14:3–9. What virtues of the Holy Spirit can you find in this story? Explain.

_____

_____

_____

_____

_____

_____

_____

_____

Living by God's Word

THE GIFTS OF THE SPIRIT

Two virtues of the Spirit that show special strength of character are faithfulness and self-control.

FAITHFULNESS

God calls us to be faithful to our Christian beliefs even when we are looked down upon by others. Jesus teaches us that we can be faithful because God is always faithful to us. Being faithful means loving the people in our lives we are given to love. It means going the extra mile out of love. Sometimes we do not see the results of our faithfulness. God calls us to trust in God's love for us, no matter what else comes our way.

In Paul's letter to the Romans, he instructs the people that God's love will never desert us. In your Bible, look up Romans 8:38—39 and reflect on the words.

Think of a time in your life when you feared that something would not turn out all right, but you trusted that it would. Or recall a time when you believed in somebody even when no one else did. What difference did your faithfulness make? Write about your experience.

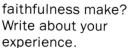

SELF-CONTROL

We are called to be people who use self-control even when it seems as if everything around us encourages us to get all that we can for ourselves. We try to have balance in all areas of our lives. Self-control helps us build strength to live the gospel message so that it becomes the foundation of all we do.

There are many ways that we can practice self-control so that we can achieve the goals we set for ourselves. To be self-controlled means not looking for the easy thing to do. Sometimes it means doing something that we may not feel like doing.

In his first letter to the people in the Greek city of Corinth, Paul compares living the Christian life to being a winning athlete who trains to be the best he or she can be. Look up 1 Corinthians 9:24—25.

Think about ways in your life in which you have disciplined yourself. What are the advantages? Think about areas in which you would like to be more disciplined. What are they? Write about your achievements and your goals.

_____

_____

_____

_____

_____

_____

REVIEWING OUR FAITH

God

What do we believe about God?

We believe that God is the all-loving Creator, the Father and Mother, of everything that exists. God is all-powerful and all-knowing, yet cares enough to look after each creature.

Is God always with us?

God is present to us in a personal way. Christians can experience God in prayer and worship, in the sacraments, and in people.

Can we fully understand God?

God is a mystery and cannot be fully understood. We are called to grow in our relationship with God and in our understanding.

What is the Trinity?

The doctrine of the Trinity tells us that there are three persons in one God: the Father, the Son, and the Holy Spirit. Through the Trinity we experience grace to be unified with God and one another, to become holy, and to enjoy eternal life.

What is grace?

The gift of God's loving life and presence shared with us is called grace.

Jesus

Who is Jesus?

Jesus is the Christ, the anointed one of God. He is both fully God and fully human. Jesus is the Son of God and the son of Mary.

Why did God send us Jesus?

God sent Jesus so that through him we can know God's healing love, receive God's forgiveness, and experience God's eternal life.

What is the Incarnation?

The mystery of the Incarnation describes how the Son of God became human in Jesus to save us from sin and death. Jesus is the Word of God who speaks and acts in our lives. Jesus reveals God's truth to us.

What is the resurrection?

God freed Jesus from death and raised him to new life. Through Jesus' death and resurrection, we, too, can share in God's eternal life.

What was Jesus' mission?

Jesus came so that all people might have new life with God. He preached and practiced obedience to God's will as the way to true peace. Jesus dedicated his life to people who suffer from illness, poverty, and injustice.

How does Jesus continue his mission?

Jesus formed a community of disciples to unite, heal, and call people to oneness with God and service to others.

Jesus promised to be with his followers always. He shares the power of his resurrection with us to strengthen us in overcoming life's difficulties.

How is Jesus with us?

Jesus shares with his followers the life that he shares with God.

Jesus sent his disciples to baptize people as a sign of new life, forgiveness, and fellowship.

Jesus calls the members of his Church to continue his mission and be signs of his presence in the world.

Holy Spirit

Who is the Holy Spirit?
The Spirit of God is called the Holy Spirit. Jesus sends the Spirit to us to help us become holy as God is holy.

How does the Spirit make us holy?
The Holy Spirit sanctifies us, or helps us become holy, by uniting us with God and one another. The Spirit helps us form a community of believers who care about one another and the world.

The Holy Spirit guides us and reconciles us to God and one another.

The Holy Spirit renews the Church to help it grow and be open to the whole world.

What are the gifts of the Spirit?
We describe the action of the Holy Spirit in our lives as the seven gifts. These are wisdom, understanding, knowledge, right judgment, courage, reverence, wonder, and awe.

Are there other gifts of the Spirit?
There are gifts of the Spirit called charismatic gifts. Some of these gifts are described in 1 Corinthians 12:7–11. They are special gifts given to Jesus' followers and are used to build up the Church.

What are the signs or virtues of the Spirit?
As we attempt to live by the power of the gifts, our lives show the virtues of the Spirit. These are love, joy, peace, patience, kindness, generosity, faithfulness, gentleness, and self-control.

Are there other virtues of the Spirit?
With the theological virtues of faith, hope, and love, the Spirit helps us form our conscience.

The cardinal virtues of prudence, justice, fortitude, and temperance are spiritual strengths that help us choose well in our relationships.

When do we receive the Holy Spirit?
The Holy Spirit comes to us at Baptism and is celebrated in our lives at Confirmation.

The Church

What do we believe about the Church?
The Church began on Pentecost with the coming of the Holy Spirit to the apostles.

The Church is a community of believers who live in and through the Holy Spirit.

The Church is Christ's Mystical Body, continuing his mission of community-building, preaching the Word, worship, and service.

What are the Church's ideals?
The Church's ideals are unity, faithfulness to Jesus' teaching, the celebration of the sacraments, and service to all, especially poor and oppressed people.

The Church expresses its faith in a rich liturgy, in strong principles of justice and compassion, and in its creeds.

The Catholic Church is universal, finding a home in various cultures.

How does the Church celebrate the presence of Christ?
The followers of Jesus celebrate his presence in their lives through prayer and the sacraments.

The Church is holy, calling us to know and love Jesus and become more like him.

How does the Church teach?

The teaching of the Church comes to us through Scripture and tradition. The Church's doctrines are rooted in the teaching of the apostles and are expressed by ecumenical councils as well as by the bishops in union with the pope. Although the basic beliefs of Christianity are unchanging, our understanding and explanation of these beliefs continues to grow as our relationship with God grows.

The Church is continually reformed and renewed by the Holy Spirit.

Christians try to identify themselves with the poor and to free all suffering people from poverty and oppression.

The Church expresses its faith in worship, in its creeds, and in the way Christian women and men live their lives.

Tradition

What is tradition?

Tradition is the way that the Church, guided by the Holy Spirit, passes on its living faith throughout history.

Tradition includes beliefs, customs, rituals, and laws by which the People of God have lived and continue to live their faith through the centuries.

Sacraments

What are the sacraments?

The sacraments are effective signs that make God's grace present to us to love, heal, and transform our lives.

The sacraments celebrate the presence of the risen Christ in our lives.

Which sacraments are called the sacraments of initiation?

Baptism, Confirmation, and the Eucharist are the sacraments of initiation into the Church.

What do we achieve through the sacraments of initiation?

Through the sacraments of initiation, we enter into new life with God and are welcomed into the community of Jesus' followers in order to live as Jesus did.

Why are Baptism, Confirmation, and the Eucharist called the sacraments of initiation?

Baptism and Confirmation celebrate the gift of the Holy Spirit who helps us share in Jesus' ministry.

Baptism celebrates the new Christian's sharing in the life of Christ.

In Confirmation, we are called to grow in faith and to witness to Christ in our words and actions.

The Eucharist recalls Christ's presence in all of life, remembers his death and resurrection, and celebrates our unity as a Church.

The Eucharist is the central celebration of the Church; through the Eucharist we are called to serve others.

What are the sacraments of forgiveness and healing?

Reconciliation, or Penance, celebrates Christ's forgiving presence in our lives. Through Reconciliation we experience ongoing conversion to the life of Christ.

In the Anointing of the Sick, the Church continues Jesus' ministry to the sick and celebrates his healing and forgiving presence.

What are the sacraments of vocation?

Marriage celebrates God's call of a woman and a man to love one another, their children, their faith community, and the world. Marriage is a sign of the love that Christ has for the Church.

Holy Orders celebrates God's call to special ministry as bishop, priest, or deacon.

Confirmation Facts

What promise did Jesus make to the apostles before he returned to the Father?

Before he returned to the Father, Jesus made this promise: "I will ask the Father, and he will give you another Advocate to be with you always, the Spirit of truth" (John 14:16–17a).

When was the promise of Jesus fulfilled?

Jesus' promise was fulfilled at Pentecost.

. . . they were all gathered in one place together. And suddenly there came from the sky a noise like a strong driving wind, and it filled the entire house in which they were. Then there appeared to them tongues as of fire, which parted and came to rest on each one of them. And they were all filled with the holy Spirit . . . .

Acts 2:1–4

How is the Holy Spirit given to the followers of Jesus?

Through Baptism, God the Father gives us a new birth by the Holy Spirit. We become the sons and daughters of God through the outpouring of the Holy Spirit.

Through Confirmation, we receive God's Spirit in a new and fuller way. The Holy Spirit helps us live as followers of Jesus and helps us bear witness to Christ as Lord.

Who may receive the sacrament of Confirmation?

Confirmation may be conferred upon any baptized Catholic. In the Western Church, it is most often conferred when a candidate wants to enter more fully into the life of Christ, has been instructed, and is willing to take an active part in the life of the Church.

Who usually confirms?

The bishop is the usual minister of Confirmation. But priests can assist the bishop, or confirm on their own.

How is the sacrament of Confirmation conferred?

The sacrament is conferred through the anointing with chrism and the words, "Be sealed with the Gift of the Holy Spirit."

The confirmed person is more closely bound to Jesus. He or she is given help to spread the love of Jesus among people.

What is the ideal way in which the sacrament of Confirmation is celebrated?

Ideally, the sacrament of Confirmation is celebrated within the Eucharist. In that way, we can see the very important connection between Confirmation and the Eucharist, which are both sacraments of initiation. At the Confirmation Mass, we hear the word of God and receive the Bread of Life. We are also sealed with the gift of the Holy Spirit.

What is the role of the sponsors?

Sponsors present the persons to be confirmed to the bishop for the anointing. They speak in the name of the whole believing community. The sponsors later help the confirmed persons witness to Christ in their daily lives.

What does Confirmation call us to be?

Confirmation calls us to be committed Christians. We are to live the message of Jesus in everyday life. The sacrament calls us to continue to pray, serve others, and celebrate with the People of God, gathered as Church.

The Bible

What is the Bible?

The Bible, or Sacred Scripture, is a collection of books that tells the story of God and God's people. The stories of the Bible span 2,000 years and were written in many different literary styles by many authors over a long period of time.

The Bible is made up of two parts—the Hebrew Scriptures, or Old Testament, and the Christian Scriptures, or New Testament.

Why is Scripture called revelation?

Sacred Scripture is called revelation because the writers of the various books were inspired by the Holy Spirit to reveal the saving word and action of God in their writings.

What are the Hebrew Scriptures?

The Hebrew Scriptures consist of 46 books, and they record God's saving word and action as spoken through the people of Israel.

What are the Christian Scriptures?

The 27 books of the Christian Scriptures tell the story of Jesus Christ and the early Church as remembered by the evangelists and leaders of the first Christian communities.

After Jesus' resurrection and ascension, Paul was the first writer of the Christian Scriptures. He mostly wrote letters to his fellow Christians.

The four gospels tell about the life, death, and resurrection of Jesus. The word *gospel* means "good news." The gospel writers are Matthew, Mark, Luke, and John.

Mary

What do we believe about Mary?

Mary is the mother of Jesus, the Son of God.

Why is she called a disciple?

Mary is called a disciple because she believed in her son, Jesus, and followed him.

What is the Visitation?

In the gospel of Luke, Mary visits her aged cousin, Elizabeth, who is awaiting the birth of John the Baptist. In her prayer of greeting, Mary is shown to be mindful of the needs of the poor.

What is meant by the Assumption?

Mary is in heaven, with body and spirit united.

Prayer

How do we pray?

Prayer is our communication with God. Prayer can be formal or informal, spoken or silent. Some traditional prayers follow this section.

Here is a description of one way to pray by meditating, or reflecting on God:

Select a short passage from one of the gospels. Read it slowly and thoughtfully a few times. Then close your eyes. Imagine yourself in the scene. Picture yourself with Jesus. Think about what he is saying and doing. Imagine that he is talking to you. What is your response?

Justice and Peace

What is our Christian call?

Christlike compassion implies a commitment to work for justice and peace for all of God's people on earth.

We are to stand with the poor in their struggle for personal freedom and responsibility.

Justice might involve changing political, economic, and cultural systems that violate the dignity and rights of people.

Our call is to free people from poverty, illiteracy, hunger, fear, and oppression.

What are some ways we are called to work for peace?

The American bishops, in their letter *The Challenge of Peace*, ask us to promote nuclear disarmament.

Likewise we are asked to promote peace within our own families, schools, and neighborhoods. This can happen when we respect other people and seek to resolve conflicts we have with them.

Morality

As Christians, how are we called to live?

All Christians are responsible for participating in the Church's renewal.

We are called to act with compassion toward all people, to live by the works of mercy.

We are called to respect God's will for every person and for created things.

How do we discover, or identify, God's call?

We learn God's will through prayer, respect for Church teachings, study of the gospel, living in Christian community, and service.

Prayers and Precepts

Prayer for the Spirit of God

Come, Holy Spirit, fill the hearts of your faithful
and kindle in them the fire of your love.
Send forth your Spirit, and they shall be recreated;
and you will renew the face of the earth.

The Greatest Commandments

"You shall love the Lord, your God, with all your heart, with all your soul, with all your mind, and with all your strength . . . .

You shall love your neighbor as yourself."

Mark 12:30–31

Shorter Act of Contrition

Lord Jesus, Son of God,
have mercy on me, a sinner.

Rite of Penance

Act of Contrition

My God,
I am sorry for my sins with all my heart.
In choosing to do wrong
and failing to do good
I have sinned against you
whom I should love above all things.
I firmly intend, with your help,
to do penance,
to sin no more,
and to avoid whatever leads me to sin.
Our Savior Jesus Christ
suffered and died for us.
In his name, my God, have mercy.

Rite of Penance

The Corporal Works of Mercy

1. Feed the hungry.
2. Give drink to the thirsty.
3. Clothe the naked.
4. Visit those in prison.
5. Shelter the homeless.
6. Visit the sick.
7. Bury the dead.

The Spiritual Works of Mercy

1. Correct sinners.
2. Teach the ignorant.
3. Give advice to those who are confused.
4. Comfort those who suffer.
5. Be patient with others.
6. Forgive injuries.
7. Pray for the living and the dead.

The Ten Commandments

1. I, the Lord, am your God. You shall not have other gods beside me.
2. You shall not take the name of the Lord, your God, in vain.
3. Remember to keep holy the sabbath day.
4. Honor your father and mother.
5. You shall not kill.
6. You shall not commit adultery.
7. You shall not steal.
8. You shall not bear false witness against your neighbor.
9. You shall not covet your neighbor's wife.
10. You shall not covet anything that belongs to your neighbor.

Based on Exodus 20:2–17
and Deuteronomy 5:6–21

Precepts of the Church

1. **To keep holy the day of the Lord's resurrection;** to worship God by participating in Mass every Sunday and holy day of obligation.

2. **To lead a sacramental life;** to receive Holy Communion frequently and the sacrament of Reconciliation regularly: minimally, to receive the sacrament of Reconciliation at least once a year. Minimally also, to receive Holy Communion at least once a year.

3. **To study Catholic teaching** in preparation for the sacrament of Confirmation, to be confirmed, and then to continue to study and advance the cause of Christ.

4. **To observe the marriage laws of the Church;** to give religious training, by example and word, to one's children; to use parish schools and catechetical programs.

5. **To strengthen and support the Church**— one's own parish community and parish priests, the worldwide Church, and the pope.

6. **To do penance, including abstaining from meat** and fasting from food on the appointed days.

7. **To join in the missionary spirit** and apostolate of the Church.

Based on Sharing the Light of Faith (NCD)

PARTS OF THE MASS

INTRODUCTORY RITES

Gathering Song

Greeting   The celebrant welcomes us and invites us to pray.

Penitential Rite   We confess our sinfulness and ask forgiveness of God and each other.

Gloria   A prayer of praise.

Opening Prayer

LITURGY OF THE WORD

First Reading   Taken from the Old Testament.

Responsorial Psalm

Second Reading   Taken from the New Testament.

Gospel Acclamation

Gospel   A reading by the priest or deacon from one of the four gospels.

Homily   An explanation of the readings given by the celebrant or deacon.

Profession of Faith   The Nicene Creed is recited.

General Intercessions (Prayer of the Faithful)   Short petitions of prayer offered for the needs of the Church and all God's people.

LITURGY OF THE EUCHARIST

Preparation of the Altar and the Gifts   The preparation for the meal as we offer our gifts to God.

Prayer over the Gifts

Eucharistic Prayer   A prayer of praise and thanksgiving during which the bread and wine become the body and blood of Jesus.

Communion Rite

　The Lord's Prayer   (Our Father)

　　Sign of Peace   We greet one another with the Lord's peace.

　Breaking of the Bread   The celebrant prepares to distribute the Eucharist as he invites us to reflect on the meal we are about to share.

　Communion

　Period of Silence or **Song of Praise**

　Prayer After Communion

CONCLUDING RITE

Greeting

Blessing

Dismissal

THE LITURGICAL YEAR

Each calendar year the Church celebrates Jesus' life, death, and resurrection in a cycle called the liturgical year.

Advent The year begins with the First Sunday of Advent. It is a season of joyful waiting.

Christmas Season We celebrate Christ's birthday, the feast of Mary, Mother of God, the Epiphany, and the Baptism of the Lord.

Lent During Lent we prepare to celebrate Easter. Lent is a forty day period of prayer and sacrifice. It begins with Ash Wednesday.

Easter Triduum Begins with the Lord's Supper on Holy Thursday. It ends with evening prayer on Easter Sunday.

Easter Season The Church continues to celebrate Christ's resurrection. Toward the end of this season we celebrate the Ascension and Pentecost.

Ordinary Time Ordinary Time consists of 33 or 34 weeks. During this time we celebrate all that Jesus has taught us, and listen to stories about his life.

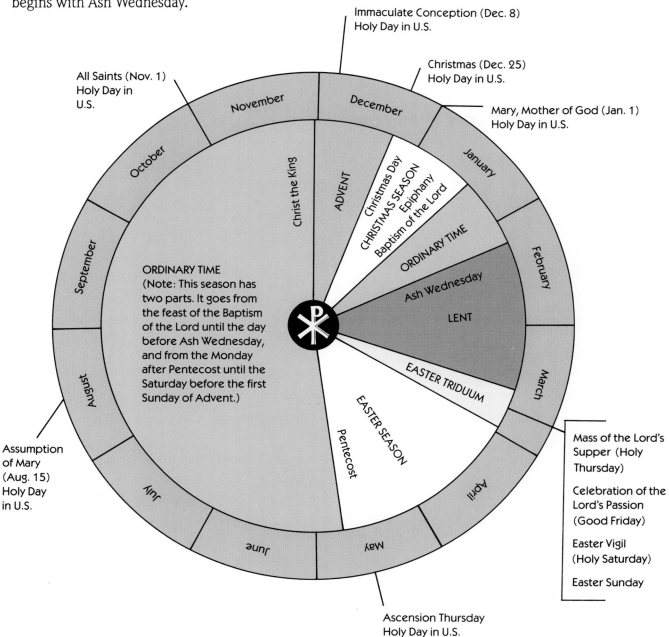

Immaculate Conception (Dec. 8)
Holy Day in U.S.

Christmas (Dec. 25)
Holy Day in U.S.

Mary, Mother of God (Jan. 1)
Holy Day in U.S.

All Saints (Nov. 1)
Holy Day in U.S.

November

December

January

October

September

August

July

June

May

April

March

February

Christ the King

ADVENT

Christmas Day
CHRISTMAS SEASON
Epiphany
Baptism of the Lord

ORDINARY TIME

Ash Wednesday

LENT

EASTER TRIDUUM

EASTER SEASON

Pentecost

ORDINARY TIME
(Note: This season has two parts. It goes from the feast of the Baptism of the Lord until the day before Ash Wednesday, and from the Monday after Pentecost until the Saturday before the first Sunday of Advent.)

Assumption of Mary (Aug. 15) Holy Day in U.S.

Mass of the Lord's Supper (Holy Thursday)

Celebration of the Lord's Passion (Good Friday)

Easter Vigil (Holy Saturday)

Easter Sunday

Ascension Thursday
Holy Day in U.S.

95

Glossary

absolution
the prayer of forgiveness for sins prayed by the priest in the sacrament of Reconciliation *p. 43*

Anointing of the Sick
the sacrament of comfort and strength, of forgiveness and healing *p. 42*

Baptism
a sacrament of initiation through which we become members of the Church *p. 6*

Beatitudes
the basic principles of life in God's kingdom *pp. 55–56*

bishop
a successor of the apostles who leads a diocese *p. 6*

Body of Christ
the Church, the community of those who are united with Christ and with one another in Christ *p. 14*

catechumen
an unbaptized person who is being initiated into the Church *p. 14*

chrism
a perfumed oil blessed by the bishop and used in the sacraments of Baptism, Confirmation, and Holy Orders *p. 7*

Confirmation
a sacrament of initiation in which we are sealed and strengthened with the gift of the Holy Spirit *p. 2*

creed
a formal summary of basic beliefs *p. 50*

diocese
a Catholic community made up of many parishes *p. 15*

Eucharist
a sacrament of initiation that celebrates the real presence of Jesus in the assembled community, in the proclamation of the word, in the consecration of the bread and wine, and in sharing Holy Communion *p. 14*

gift of the Spirit
the power given by the Holy Spirit at Baptism and strengthened at Confirmation to help us live as Christians (*See also* seven gifts of the Spirit) *p. 29*

Holy Orders
the sacrament of service in which men are ordained to serve the Church by preaching, celebrating the sacraments, and building a more just community *p. 43*

homily
a talk about the readings at Mass *p. 15*

inspiration
God's guidance of the writers of the Bible so that their words were really God's word *p. 39*

liturgy
the Church's official public worship *p. 18*

Marriage
the sacrament that celebrates the promise of lifelong love between a man and a woman *p. 43*

Pentecost
the day the Church began when the Holy Spirit came upon the apostles *p. 15*

Reconciliation

a sacrament that celebrates in a special way the love and forgiveness of God, brings us healing and peace, and reconciles us with God and with the Christian community *p. 42*

revelation

God's speaking to us about God, about ourselves, and about the world; God's revelation is still going on *p. 41*

Rite of Christian Initiation

the process of religious education and liturgical celebration through which one is prepared for full sacramental life in the Church *p. 14*

sacraments of initiation

visible signs of invisible grace or signs of sacred reality that enable one to become a full member of the Body of Christ; Baptism, Confirmation, and Eucharist *p. 14*

seven gifts of the Spirit

wisdom, understanding, knowledge, right judgment, courage, reverence, wonder, and awe *p. 61–62*

signs of the Spirit

qualities, or virtues, in our lives that show we are living by the gifts of the Spirit: love, joy, peace, patience, kindness, generosity, faithfulness, gentleness, self-control *p. 67*

sponsor

a baptized, confirmed Catholic who models Christian living for the Confirmation candidate and presents the candidate to the bishop *p. 18*

witness

one who tells or shows what he or she has seen or heard *p. 19*

© 1986 "Pentecost/Salvation Suite" by William Schickel

Index